STUFFED EGGPLANTS
(see page 24)

GOULASH WITH NOODLES
(see page 114)

CASSEROLE
COOKBOOK

Photography, Reg Morrison
Food for Photography,
Elizabeth Sewell, Judy Barr
Design, Hugh M‘Leod

Published by Paul Hamlyn Pty. Ltd.
176 South Creek Road
Dee Why West, New South Wales 2099
© Copyright Paul Hamlyn Pty. Ltd. 1971
ISBN 0 600 07078 6
First Published 1972
Printed by Lee Fung, Hong Kong

CASSEROLE COOKBOOK

Elizabeth Sewell

Paul Hamlyn
Sydney, London, New York, Toronto

Introduction

Casserole Cookbook takes its name from a cooking utensil — a lidded heatproof pot that dates back for centuries to its most primitive form — the wrapping of meat in clay to protect it from the fierce heat of the fire.

European cooks have developed the use of the casserole until it is now the most versatile and convenient way of cooking many different types of food — meat, poultry, fish, eggs and vegetables.

The casserole is the housewife's best friend. In it, she can prepare an infinite variety of dishes, from simple, but delicious family meals, to the main course for an elegant dinner party. At the same time, she can prove herself a superb cook.

One of the chief pleasures of casserole cookery is its convenience and simplicity. All preparation can be done in advance — indeed many casseroles gain in flavour from being cooked a day or so ahead and then reheated. This means a minimum of work and washing up. The food is cooked and served in the one dish or with the preliminary use of one saucepan or frying pan if the casserole is not flameproof. There are economic advantages also. The cheaper cuts of meat ideally suited for casserole cookery can be made even more tender and flavoursome by marinating for several hours before cooking. The addition of vegetables, herbs and spices, produce delicious meals with complete nutritive value. With this method of cooking, fuel costs are low and food values high.

For entertaining, more elaborate casseroles can be prepared and served with equal ease. What a joy for the working wife or the busy mother of a family! With her casserole safely in the oven, simmering in all its delicious goodness she can relax and enjoy herself, having no worries about split second timing and serving. For this reason, approximate times only have been given for the cooking time for each casserole in this book. The casserole can be cooked for a long period at a low temperature, but should the meal be required earlier than expected, the temperature can be raised and cooking accelerated with no harm done.

Contents

Guide to Weights and Measures

The weights and fluid measures used throughout this book refer to those of THE STANDARDS ASSOCIATION OF AUSTRALIA. All spoon measurements are level unless otherwise stated. A good set of scales, a graduated Australian Standard measuring cup and a set of Australian Standard measuring spoons will be most helpful. These are available at leading hardware stores.

The Australian Standard measuring cup has a capacity of 8 fluid ounces.
The Australian Standard tablespoon has a capacity of 20 millilitres.
The Australian Standard teaspoon has a capacity of 5 millilitres.
The British imperial pint (used in Australia) has a volume of 20 fluid ounces.

AMERICAN AND CANADIAN WEIGHTS

AMERICAN weights and measures are the same except for the tablespoon and the pint.
Housewives in AMERICA and CANADA using this book should remember that the AUSTRALIAN standard measuring tablespoon has a capacity of 20 millilitres, whereas the AMERICAN/CANADIAN standard measuring tablespoon has a capacity of 15 millilitres, therefore all tablespoon measures should be taken generously in AMERICA and CANADA.
It is also important to know that the imperial pint (20 fluid ounces) is used in Australia, whereas the AMERICAN/CANADIAN pint has a volume of 16 fluid ounces.

Metric Guide

Because there is no exact conversion between metric and imperial units, we suggest the housewife replaces 1 ounce with 25 grams and 1 fluid ounce with 25 millilitres.

In order to preserve the correct ratio of ingredients in a recipe, strict conversion should not be applied. Each imperial measure — whether a pound, pint or cup, should be related to the base unit of the imperial system — the ounce or fluid ounce. The number of ounces and fluid ounces should be multiplied by 25 to give the metric quantities, thereby preserving the proportions.

This has been done in the table provided.

Ounces and Fluid Ounces	Grams and Millilitres
1	25
2	50
3	75
4	100
5	125
6	150
7	175
8	200
10	250
12	300
16 (1 pound)	400
20 (1 pint)	500

Liquid proportions should be adjusted if necessary to maintain correct consistencies.

Metric Usage follows Metric Conversion Board Recommendation.

Oven Temperature Guide

This is an approximate guide only. Different makes of stoves vary and even the same make of stove can give slightly different individual results at the same temperature. If in doubt with your particular stove, do refer to your own manufacturer's temperature chart. It is impossible in a general book to be exact for every stove, but the following is a good average guide in every case.

The following chart also gives approximate conversions from degrees Fahrenheit to degrees Celsius (formerly known as Centigrade). This chart can be used for conversion of recipes which give oven temperatures in metric measures.

| | Thermostat Setting | | |
	°F		°C
Description of Oven	Automatic Electric	Gas	
Cool	200	200	100
Very slow	250	250	120
Slow	300-325	300	150-160
Moderately slow	325-350	325	160-170
Moderate	350-375	350	170-190
Moderately hot	375-400	375	190-200
Hot	400-450	400	200-230
Very hot	450-500	450	230-260

CHOICE
AND CARE OF
CASSEROLES

The ideal casserole cooks well and looks well. Today there is an almost bewildering variety from which to choose.

Materials vary greatly, and prices too, so it is sensible to put some thought into the choice of your casseroles.

There are four main points to remember:
The weight of the casserole is an indication of its thickness, which is necessary for slow even cooking.

The size of the casserole is also important. A small amount of food should be cooked in a small casserole. This will prevent food from drying out and losing delicious flavour and juices. Choose larger casseroles for party casserole recipes. Roughly speaking, a 1-2 pint casserole holds a meal for 1 or 2 people, a 2-3 pint casserole for 2 to 4, and a 3-4½ pint casserole for 4 to 6. So select your casserole with the size of your family in mind, and 'splash' with an outsize one for parties.

Thirdly, if the casserole is labelled 'flameproof', you can use it safely on the top of the stove for the preliminary cooking which is a great advantage.

Finally, attractive design and colour are important as the casserole goes straight from kitchen to table.

Other points to notice are that the lid is well fitting and that handles are designed to give a good grasp when the casserole is hot and full.

Next, consider the various materials, they range from the most elegant ovenproof china to rustic earthenware.

All types of earthenware are most attractive and are great favourites with French cooks. Some are very reasonable in price, they are good conductors of heat and are heavy enough without being difficult to handle when full. However, they are not suitable to use on top of the stove and they are breakable.

Cast iron casseroles with vitreous enamelled exteriors and interiors are a popular choice. They are expensive, but they are flameproof, well designed, easy to clean and practically everlasting.

Plain cast iron casseroles cook just as well, but food should never be stored in them. They should be perfectly dry and coated with a little oil before being put away, otherwise rust may appear on the surface.

Lighter types of metal, such as aluminium, are often used as a base for enamelled casseroles and are excellent for stove-top use. Make sure the enamel is of good quality to minimise the risk of chipping.

Copper looks beautiful and is the choice of chefs because of its lasting qualities and because it is the best know conductor of heat, but good quality copper is expensive and is difficult to keep clean without scouring and polishing.

With ovenproof glass, one can see the food cooking — a great advantage — and it is inexpensive and easy to clean. However, it is liable to crack with sudden changes of temperature, so a cold casserole should never be put into a hot oven, neither should cold liquids be poured into a hot casserole. The newest form of glass cookware is glass ceram. It has none of these disadvantages — it can be put straight from the refrigerator into a hot oven and is not easily broken if dropped.

As you can see, there is a casserole for every possible occasion, from the family barbecue to the formal dinner party, and they are as good to look at as they are to use.

One last point, make sure you have heatproof mats to put under your casserole when you bring it to the table!

CARE OF CASSEROLES

A well designed casserole, with no crevices where food can

stick and bake on, is simple to keep clean. Let the dish stand full of water for several hours and food will clean off easily. Never scour cast iron, just use hot water and a little detergent, and never use any abrasives on non-stick surfaces. Use a nylon scourer, not steel wool, for stubborn spots on other types, but you will find that most stains will wash off after overnight soaking. A weak solution of household bleach and water may be used on glass and enamel-surfaced casseroles if they are badly stained, but this should not happen if a little care is taken from the beginning.

Terms used in Casserole Cookbook

Beurre Manié: A paste made from equal parts of butter and flour, used to thicken some casseroles.

Bouquet Garni: A bunch of herbs, used to flavour casseroles and stews. Usually consists of sprigs of parsley, thyme, marjoram, rosemary, a bay leaf, peppercorns and cloves, tied together in a piece of muslin.

Capsicum: Pepper.

Casserole: A cooking utensil with a lid, made of earthenware, glazed china or metal, it is often used for food which requires long slow cooking.

Coat: To cover entire surface with a mixture such as seasoned flour, breadcrumbs, batter, or to cover vegetables with sauce.

Cornflour: Cornstarch.

Croûte: A round or oval piece of bread, fried or toasted. Used to garnish casseroles.

Eggplant: Aubergine.

French Beans: Green beans, string beans.

Frying Pan: Skillet.

Grill: To broil.

Marinade: Usually a mixture of an oil, acid and seasonings in which food is marinated to give it more flavour and to soften the tissues of tough food.

Marinate: To let food stand in a marinade.

Minced Steak: Ground beef.

Plain Flour: All-purpose flour.

Ragoût: A stew made from regular sized pieces of meat, poultry or fish, sautéed in fat until brown and then simmered with stock, meat juices or water, or a combination of these, until tender.

Ramekin: Individual baking dish.

Reduce:	To cook a sauce over a high heat, uncovered, until it is reduced by evaporation to the desired consistency. This culinary process improves both flavour and appearance.
Sauté:	To fry lightly in a small amount of hot fat or oil, shaking the pan or turning food frequently during cooking, usually until the fat or oil is absorbed.
Seasoned Flour:	Plain flour to which salt and pepper have been added. It is used for coating meat and fish before frying or stewing.
Simmer:	To cook in liquid just below boiling point, with small bubbles rising occasionally to the surface.
Spring Onion:	Shallot or scallion.
Stew:	A long slow method of cooking in a covered pan in a small amount of liquid, usually to tenderize tough meat.
Stock:	A liquid containing the flavours, extracts and nutrients of bones, meat, fish or vegetables in which they are cooked.
Stock Cube:	Bouillon cube.
Zucchini:	Courgette.

FAMILY CASSEROLES

Here is a collection of well tested traditional family favourites. Delicious, hearty casseroles all the family will enjoy. No need to worry when an extra schoolfriend stays for dinner—these are 'stretchy' meals. Beef, lamb, pork, poultry and fish—there are casseroles here which will please every member of your family.

Carbonnade of Beef

Time: 1¾-2 hours
Temperature: 350-375° F
Serves: 4-5

2 lb blade steak
1-2 tablespoons dripping
8 oz onions, sliced
1 tablespoon (½ oz) plain flour
1 clove garlic, crushed
1¼ cups beer
1¼ cups water
bouquet garni
salt and pepper
pinch of freshly grated nutmeg
pinch of sugar
1 teaspoon vinegar
4-5 slices bread, ¼x2x2-inches
French mustard

Remove fat from meat and cut into 2-inch pieces. Heat dripping in a flameproof casserole and brown meat quickly. Remove from casserole, add onion and cook until lightly browned. Add flour and garlic, stir until well blended. Add all remaining ingredients except bread and French mustard and replace meat in casserole. Cover and simmer gently in a moderate oven for approximately 1½ hours or until meat is tender.

Spread bread with mustard and place on top of meat in casserole, push bread down below the surface making sure it is soaked with gravy. Place uncovered casserole back in oven for a further 15-20 minutes or until bread has floated to the top again and is crisp and brown.

INGREDIENTS FOR SPANISH DUCK
(see page 35)

OLD FASHIONED FISH PIE
(see page 52)

Beef Olives

Time: approximately 1½ hours
Temperature: 300-325° F
Serves: 4

1-1½ lb lean topside steak
4 rashers bacon
4 tablespoons (2 oz) seasoned flour
2 tablespoons dripping
½ cup water
½ cup red wine
½ cup tomato juice
2 tablespoons apple or redcurrant jelly
1 tablespoon vinegar
1 teaspoon grated lemon rind
1 teaspoon ground cloves
1 tablespoon (½ oz) cornflour blended with 1 tablespoon cold
   water (optional)

Cut steak into thin slices, flatten with a meat mallet until
¼-inch thick. Cut into 4-inch squares. Remove rind from bacon
and cut into pieces, place bacon on steak and roll up neatly,
tie with string. Dip Beef Olives in seasoned flour.

Heat dripping in a flameproof casserole and brown meat
evenly on all sides. Add all remaining ingredients except
blended cornflour, cover and cook in a slow oven for
approximately 1½ hours or until meat is tender.

Remove string from meat before serving and thicken gravy
with blended cornflour if desired. Adjust seasoning and serve
with baked jacket potatoes and a green vegetable.

Note: Beef Olives are even more delicious if made the day
before and reheated.

Pot Roast

Time: approximately 2½ hours
Serves: 5-6

2 large carrots
2 large parsnips
5-6 onions
3 tablespoons dripping
1x3-4 lb corner piece topside steak
salt
freshly ground pepper
boiling water
mustard or horseradish relish for serving

Peel vegetables and cut carrots and parsnips into 3-4 pieces.

Heat dripping in a large flameproof casserole, brown meat evenly on all sides. Remove meat from casserole and brown vegetables in remaining fat, remove from casserole.

Replace meat in casserole, season with salt and pepper and add 2 tablespoons boiling water. Cover casserole with greased paper or aluminium foil and a tight fitting lid. Cook over a gentle heat for approximately 2½ hours or until meat is tender, adding 2 tablespoons boiling water to casserole every 30 minutes. Add vegetables 1½ hours before cooking time is completed.

Serve Pot Roast with mustard or horseradish relish and gravy from casserole if liked.

Note: Chicken, rabbit, breast of veal or mutton may be cooked in the same way.

Steak Casserole with Parsley Dumplings

Time: 2 hours
Temperature: 350-375° F
Serves: 4-5

2 lb blade steak
¼ teaspoon freshly grated nutmeg
1 teaspoon brown sugar
1 teaspoon salt
pinch of pepper
1 tablespoon (½ oz) plain flour
2 cups beef stock or water and beef stock cubes
1 tablespoon vinegar
1 tablespoon Worcestershire sauce
8-10 small white onions
2 carrots, cut into ½-inch rings

Parsley Dumplings:
1 cup (4 oz) self-raising flour
1 teaspoon salt
pinch of pepper
½ oz butter or margarine
1 tablespoon finely chopped parsley
milk

Remove fat from steak and cut into 1½-inch pieces. Combine nutmeg, sugar, salt, pepper and flour and dip meat in seasoned flour. Place in an ovenproof casserole and add stock, vinegar and Worcestershire sauce. Cover and cook in a moderate oven for 1 hour.

Add onions and carrots, return to oven and cook for a further 1 hour or until meat is tender. Place dumplings on top of meat in casserole for last 25 minutes of cooking time. Serve casserole with a green vegetable.

Parsley Dumplings: Sieve flour, salt and pepper into a mixing bowl. Rub in butter and add parsley. Add enough milk to form a soft dough. Shape dough into 8-10 small balls.

Sweet and Sour Steak

Time: 1-1½ hours
Temperature: 350-375° F
Serves: 4

1½ lb blade steak
2 tablespoons (1 oz) seasoned flour
2 tablespoons oil
1 tablespoon finely chopped root ginger
1 x 15 oz can pineapple pieces
3 stalks celery, sliced
1 onion, chopped
1 large tomato, skinned and chopped
½ cup brown vinegar
2 tablespoons (1 oz) sugar
2 teaspoons soya sauce
boiled rice for serving

Cut steak into 1-inch pieces, dip in seasoned flour. Heat oil in a flameproof casserole and brown meat evenly. Add remaining ingredients and stirring occasionally, bring to simmering point.

Cover casserole, place in a moderate oven and cook 1-1½ hours or until meat is tender. Serve with boiled rice.

Note: For a more economical casserole, make with minced steak. Cook in a moderate oven for 1 hour.

Meat Balls Romanoff

Time: 50 minutes
Temperature: 375-400° F
reducing to 300-325° F
Serves: 3-4

1 onion, finely chopped
1 tablespoon vegetable oil
1 lb finely minced steak
1 egg
salt and pepper
1 tablespoon prepared horseradish relish
½ cup crushed breakfast cereal
½ oz butter or margarine
1 tablespoon (½ oz) plain flour
1 cup sour cream
1 tablespoon tomato paste
extra salt and pepper
green peas for serving

Sauté onion in hot oil until tender and golden, drain. In a mixing bowl, combine onion, minced steak, egg, salt and pepper, horseradish relish and breakfast cereal. Mix together thoroughly and shape into small balls. Place in a greased shallow ovenproof casserole and cook in a moderately hot oven for 30 minutes.

Meanwhile, melt butter in a small saucepan, add flour and stirring continuously, cook for 1 minute. Add sour cream and tomato paste, mix together thoroughly. Season to taste with extra salt and pepper.

Remove meat balls from oven and pour off any fat. Pour sauce over meat balls and cook in a slow oven for a further 20 minutes. Serve with green peas.

Shepherd's Pie

Time: 20-30 minutes
Temperature: 400-450° F
Serves: 4

1½ lb old potatoes
3 oz butter or margarine
2 tablespoons hot milk
salt
freshly ground pepper
1 onion, finely chopped
1 lb minced steak or lamb, cooked
¼ cup stock or gravy
extra salt and pepper

Peel potatoes and cook in boiling salted water until tender. Drain well and mash with 2 oz of the butter and milk, season to taste with salt and pepper, keep warm.

Meanwhile, in a flameproof casserole, heat remaining butter and sauté onion until golden. Add meat and stock, season to taste with extra salt and pepper, mix thoroughly and remove from heat. Level surface of meat with a spatula and place creamed potato on top, spread to edges of casserole.

Bake in a hot oven for 20-30 minutes or until hot and golden brown on top.

Note: Shepherd's Pie is delicious made with fresh minced steak. Cook for approximately 15 minutes in a flameproof casserole on top of stove, before covering with potato and placing in oven.

Welsh Casserole

Time: 1-1¼ hours
Temperature: 350-375° F
Serves: 4

1½ lb minced steak
1 teaspoon salt
freshly ground pepper
1 tablespoon finely chopped parsley
1 tablespoon tomato sauce
1 tablespoon Worcestershire sauce
2 tablespoons (1 oz) plain flour
1 tablespoon dripping
2 onions, thinly sliced
1 teaspoon curry powder
1 tablespoon vinegar
1 cup water
extra salt and pepper
1 cooking apple
boiled potatoes for serving

In a large mixing bowl, combine minced steak with salt, pepper,
parsley, tomato sauce, Worcestershire sauce and 1 tablespoon
of the flour. Mix thoroughly and shape into 8-10 balls.

Heat dripping in a flameproof casserole and fry meat balls until
evenly brown. Remove from casserole and sauté onion in
remaining fat until golden brown. Add remaining flour and
curry powder to casserole, blend until smooth. Add vinegar
and water and stirring continuously, bring to the boil. Season
to taste with extra salt and pepper. Replace meat balls in
casserole, cover and cook in a moderate oven for approximately
45 minutes.

Meanwhile, peel, core and slice apple. Remove casserole from
oven, add apple, cover and cook for a further 15-30 minutes.
Serve with boiled potatoes.

Stuffed Eggplants

Delicious served as an entrée or a main course

Time: approximately 45 minutes
Temperature: 350-375° F
Serves: 4

8 small eggplants
1 oz butter or margarine
1 onion, finely chopped
1 lb minced steak
1 tablespoon finely chopped parsley
½ teaspoon mixed spice
salt
freshly ground pepper
1 tomato, chopped
¼ cup water
1 egg
¼ cup milk
½ cup grated Cheddar cheese
extra salt and pepper

Cut eggplants in halves lengthways, scoop out centres and chop. Melt half the butter in a saucepan, add onion, chopped eggplant, minced steak, parsley and seasonings. Cook for 10-15 minutes, stirring occasionally. Remove from heat and divide mixture between halved eggplants.

Melt remaining butter and mix with tomato and water and pour into a large shallow ovenproof casserole. Arrange halved eggplants in a single layer in casserole. Bake in a moderate oven for 30 minutes.

Meanwhile, beat egg and milk together, add cheese and season to taste with extra salt and pepper. Remove casserole from oven and place some cheese mixture on top of each eggplant. Return to oven for approximately 15 minutes or until eggplants are tender and cheese is golden brown on top. Serve immediately.

Monaco Casserole

Time: 55 minutes - 1 hour
Temperature: 350-375° F
Serves: 4

8 oz frankfurters
8 oz lean shoulder of veal
1 tablespoon (½ oz) plain flour
salt and pepper
2 tablespoons vegetable oil
2 onions, chopped
1 cup stock or water and beef stock cube
1 large tomato, skinned and sliced
1 tablespoon finely chopped parsley
8 oz spaghetti, cooked
¼ cup grated Cheddar cheese
extra chopped parsley for garnish

Remove skin from frankfurters and cut into ¾-inch pieces. Cut veal into ½-1-inch pieces. Toss both in flour seasoned with salt and pepper.

Heat oil in a flameproof casserole, sauté onion until golden brown, remove from casserole. Lightly brown frankfurters and veal in remaining oil. Return onion to casserole and add stock, tomato and parsley. Mix together thoroughly. Cover casserole and cook in a moderate oven for 40-45 minutes.

Remove casserole from oven, add spaghetti and mix together. Adjust seasonings if necessary and sprinkle casserole with grated cheese. Return to oven for a further 15 minutes or until hot and cheese is golden brown on top. Garnish with chopped parsley before serving.

Veal Escalopes

Time: 1 hour
Temperature: 300-325° F
Serves: 4

4 escalopes veal
seasoned flour
1 egg, beaten
dry breadcrumbs for coating
2 oz butter or margarine
8 oz mushrooms, sliced
1 cup tomato sauce
¾ cup chicken stock or water and chicken stock cube
2 oz almonds, slivered and toasted
pinch each of oregano, thyme and rosemary
salt and pepper
4 thick slices ham, cooked
buttered noodles or creamed potatoes for serving

Dip veal in seasoned flour, then beaten egg and finally coat
with breadcrumbs.

Heat butter in a frying pan and fry veal quickly on both sides
until golden brown. Remove from pan and place on absorbent
paper. Sauté mushrooms in remaining butter for 5 minutes,
add tomato sauce, stock, almonds, herbs and season to taste
with salt and pepper. Simmer for 5-10 minutes.

Place veal in an ovenproof casserole, cover with slices of ham
and pour sauce over. Cover casserole and place in a slow oven
for approximately 1 hour or until veal is tender. Serve Veal
Escalopes with buttered noodles or creamed potatoes.

Veal Paprika

Time: approximately 1¼ hours
Temperature: 350-375° F
Serves: 4-6

4 oz butter or margarine
2 onions, chopped
1 clove garlic, crushed
1½ cups beef stock or water and beef stock cubes
2 teaspoons French mustard
1 tablespoon paprika pepper
¼ cup finely chopped parsley
2 lb lean veal steak
¾ cup (3 oz) plain flour
salt
freshly ground pepper
¾ cup sour cream
2 oz blanched almonds, slivered
1x6¾ oz can champignons, drained
boiled rice or buttered new potatoes for serving

Melt half the butter in a flameproof casserole, add onions and
garlic, sauté until golden brown.

Meanwhile, in a mixing bowl, combine stock, mustard, paprika
pepper and parsley, add drained onions and garlic.

Slice veal thinly and dip in flour. Add remaining butter to
casserole and when hot, fry veal until lightly browned on both
sides. Add seasonings and stock mixture. Cover casserole and
cook in a moderate oven for approximately 1 hour or until
veal is tender.

Remove from oven, add sour cream, almonds and champignons,
stir thoroughly. Replace casserole in oven for 15 minutes but
do not allow to boil. Serve with boiled rice or buttered new
potatoes.

Note: This is an ideal party dish as it can be prepared in
advance. Add sour cream, almonds and champignons on the
day of the party and reheat gently.

Casserole of Lamb Chops

A quick and easy meal all the family will enjoy.

Time: approximately 45 minutes
Temperature: 350-375° F
Serves: 4

4 forequarter lamb chops
salt and pepper
2 onions, sliced
2 tablespoons lemon juice
1 tablespoon Worcestershire sauce
3 tablespoons tomato sauce
¾ cup stock or water and beef stock cube

Trim excess fat from chops, place in a shallow ovenproof casserole.

Season with salt and pepper and cover with onion. Combine remaining ingredients and pour over chops.

Cover casserole and cook in a moderate oven for approximately 45 minutes or until chops are tender. Serve with baked jacket potatoes and a green vegetable.

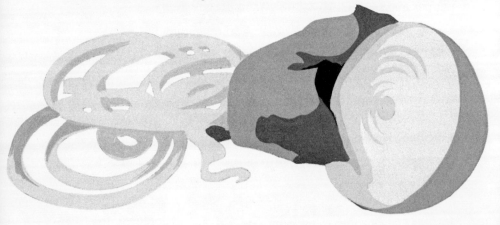

Viennese Cutlets

Time: 15-20 minutes
Temperature: 350-375° F
Serves: 4

8 lamb cutlets
2 oz butter or bacon fat
2 thick pork sausages
2 tablespoons dry breadcrumbs
salt
freshly ground pepper
1 sprig each of parsley, thyme and marjoram
2 spring onions
1 tablespoon (½ oz) plain flour
1 egg
1x15 oz can tomato purée
extra salt and pepper
pinch of sugar
creamed potato for serving

Trim cutlets. Melt half the butter in a frying pan and brown cutlets on one side only, cool on plate.

Skin sausages, place in a mixing bowl with breadcrumbs and seasonings, mix thoroughly. Finely chop herbs and spring onions and add to mixture with flour. Add beaten egg to bind mixture together. Cover cooked side of each cutlet with mixture, spreading with a wet knife.

Place cutlets in a greased shallow ovenproof casserole, forcemeat side up. Melt remaining butter and pour over cutlets. Cook in a moderate oven for 15-20 minutes or until cutlets are tender.

Meanwhile, heat tomato purée in a saucepan and season to taste with salt, pepper and sugar. Serve cutlets with tomato purée and creamed potato.

Lamb Stew

Time: 1½ hours
Temperature: 350-375° F
Serves: 6

1 x 4 lb leg of lamb, boned
2 tablespoons oil
2 tablespoons (1 oz) plain flour
2 cups water
2 tablespoons tomato paste
1 clove garlic, crushed
salt and pepper
bouquet garni
4 oz button mushrooms
3 small carrots, sliced
12 button onions
1 teaspoon sugar
6 even sized potatoes, peeled
4 tablespoons dry sherry
1 cup peas, cooked
2 tablespoons chopped parsley

Cut lamb into 1½-inch pieces.

Heat oil in a frying pan, add meat and brown evenly. Drain off fat and reserve. Sprinkle flour over lamb and stir until flour has been absorbed. Add water, tomato paste and garlic. Bring to the boil, simmer gently for 5 minutes, season to taste with salt and pepper and pour into an ovenproof casserole. Add bouquet garni, cover and simmer gently in a moderate oven for 30 minutes, remove bouquet garni.

Heat reserved fat in frying pan and sauté mushrooms for approximately 5 minutes, drain and add to ingredients in casserole. Add carrots and onions to frying pan, sprinkle with sugar and glaze quickly. Add to ingredients in casserole with potatoes, cover and cook for a further 1 hour or until lamb is tender and potatoes cooked.

Add sherry and peas to casserole just before serving and sprinkle with chopped parsley.

Spiced Lamb

Time: approximately 2 hours
Temperature: 350-375° F
Serves: 4-6

1x3 lb shoulder of lamb, boned and rolled
3 cloves garlic, slivered
1 tablespoon (½ oz) plain flour
1 teaspoon Worcestershire sauce
1 tablespoon lemon juice
2 tablespoons olive oil
2 teaspoons finely chopped mint
½ teaspoon paprika pepper
½ teaspoon salt
1 tablespoon (½ oz) sugar
¼ teaspoon freshly grated nutmeg
2 tablespoons dripping

Ask butcher to trim excess fat from meat before rolling. Make small incisions over surface of joint and insert pieces of garlic. Combine all remaining ingredients, except dripping, in a small bowl and mix together to form a smooth paste.

Heat dripping in a flameproof casserole and brown meat evenly all over. Remove from casserole and with a knife, smooth paste over surface of meat. Return meat to casserole, cover and cook in a moderate oven for approximately 2 hours or until meat is tender. Baste occasionally while cooking.

Note: If gravy is desired, place meat in a warm place and pour most of the fat from the casserole leaving approximately 2 tablespoonsful. Sprinkle 1 tablespoon (½ oz) plain flour into casserole and blend until smooth. Add ½ pint stock or vegetable water and stirring continuously, bring to the boil. Season to taste with salt and pepper and simmer 2-3 minutes. Carve meat and pour a little gravy over. Serve remaining gravy in a gravy boat.

Casserole of Pork Chops

Time: approximately 1 hour
Temperature: 350-375°F
Serves: 4

4 pork chops
1 tablespoon oil
1 large onion, sliced
1 clove garlic, crushed
1x16 oz can condensed tomato soup
¼ cup dry sherry
½ teaspoon curry powder
½ teaspoon dried sweet basil
salt
freshly ground pepper
pinch of sugar

Trim rind and excess fat from chops. Heat oil in a flameproof casserole and brown chops evenly on both sides, remove from casserole. Sauté onion and garlic in remaining fat until onion is tender. Add remaining ingredients and adjust seasonings if necessary. Replace chops in casserole.

Cook casserole, uncovered, in a moderate oven for approximately 1 hour or until chops are tender. Serve with new potatoes tossed in butter and chopped parsley and a green vegetable.

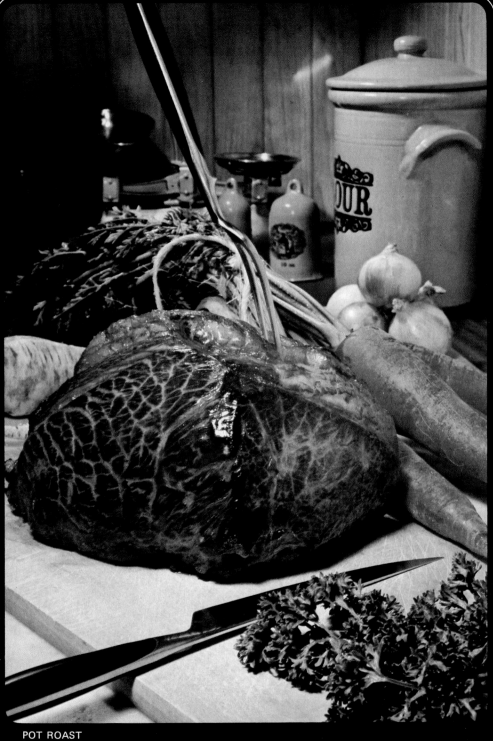

POT ROAST
(see page 18)

VEAL AND PORK CASSEROLE

Savoury Sausages

A quick and economical family meal.

Time: 15-20 minutes
Temperature: 350-375° F
Serves: 4

1 cup rice
1x15 oz can pineapple pieces
1 oz butter or margarine
1 onion, finely chopped
1 carrot, finely chopped
1 green capsicum, seeded and chopped
¼ cup tomato sauce
1 tablespoon (½ oz) brown sugar
1 lb thin pork sausages

Cook rice in boiling salted water until tender, drain and rinse well. Drain pineapple, reserve juice.

Melt butter in a frying pan, add onion, carrot and capsicum, sauté for 5 minutes, add pineapple pieces and cook for a further 5 minutes. Add tomato sauce, reserved pineapple juice and sugar, mix together thoroughly and simmer for 10 minutes.

Fry or grill sausages until golden brown all over. Place rice in an even layer in the base of a greased ovenproof casserole, arrange sausages on top and pour sauce over. Cook in a moderate oven for 15-20 minutes or until hot. Serve immediately.

Chicken in Wine Sauce

Time: approximately 1 hour
Temperature: 325-350° F
Serves: 6

2 tablespoons oil
2 oz butter or margarine
6 chicken portions
1 cup chopped onion
1 cup sliced celery
1 cup sliced carrot
1x16 oz can peeled tomatoes
1x5 oz can tomato paste
¾ cup dry white wine
2 whole cloves
pinch of ground cinnamon
2 teaspoons salt
freshly ground pepper
12 oz shell noodles

Heat oil and butter in a flameproof casserole, brown chicken pieces evenly all over. Remove from casserole and set aside. In remaining fat, sauté onion, celery and carrot for approximately 5 minutes, stir occasionally. Add tomatoes, tomato paste, wine and seasonings. Bring to the boil, mix thoroughly. Replace chicken in casserole, cover and cook in a moderately slow oven for approximately 1 hour or until chicken is tender.

Meanwhile, cook noodles in boiling salted water until tender, drain thoroughly. To serve, place noodles in a deep serving dish, arrange chicken pieces on top and pour sauce over.

Spanish Duck

Time: 1½ hours
Temperature: 375-400° F
   reducing to 350-375° F
Serves: 4

1x3 lb duck
2 oz lard
1 pint stock or water and chicken stock cubes
1 bay leaf
sprig of fresh thyme
pinch of ground mace
salt and pepper
8 small white onions
2 carrots, peeled and halved
2 stalks celery, cut into 3-inch pieces
2 tomatoes, skinned and quartered
8 even sized new potatoes
2 tablespoons (¾ oz) cornflour
¼ cup sherry
triangles of fried bread and parsley sprigs for garnish

Cut duck into serving portions.

Heat lard in a large flameproof casserole, brown pieces of duck evenly all over. Remove fat from casserole. Add stock, bay leaf, thyme and seasonings, cover and simmer gently in a moderately hot oven for 30 minutes.

Add vegetables to casserole, lower oven temperature to moderate and cook for a further 1 hour or until duck and vegetables are tender. Blend cornflour and sherry together until smooth, add to casserole and simmer for a further 3-4 minutes on top of stove. Adjust seasonings if necessary and serve casserole garnished with triangles of fried bread and parsley sprigs.

Rabbit Casserole

Time: 1 hour
Temperature: 350-375° F
Serves: 4

1 young rabbit
2 tablespoons (1 oz) plain flour
2 tablespoons bacon fat
4 rashers bacon
1 onion, finely chopped
3-4 oz mushrooms, sliced (optional)
extra 1 tablespoon (½ oz) plain flour
2 cups milk or 1 cup milk and 1 cup water
4 tablespoons tomato sauce
salt and pepper

Wipe rabbit thoroughly with a damp cloth and cut into
serving pieces, dip in flour. Melt bacon fat in a flameproof
casserole and brown rabbit evenly on all sides, remove from
casserole. Remove rind from bacon and cut each rasher in
half, fry in casserole, remove. Fry chopped onion and
mushrooms in remaining bacon fat until lightly coloured.
Add extra flour and blend until smooth. Add milk and
stirring continuously, bring to the boil. Add tomato sauce and
salt and pepper to taste. Replace rabbit and bacon in casserole
and cover.

Place casserole in a moderate oven and simmer gently for
1 hour or until rabbit is tender.

Piquant Fish Bake

Time: 35-40 minutes
Temperature: 350-375° F
Serves: 4

1 oz butter or margarine
1 tablespoon chopped onion
2 tablespoons (1 oz) plain flour
1½ cups chopped tomatoes
2 tablespoons chopped green capsicum
1 teaspoon salt
pinch of cayenne pepper
pinch of dry mustard
2 cups cooked rice
1-1½ lb fish fillets (bream or flathead)
juice of ½ lemon
finely chopped parsley for garnish

Melt butter in a saucepan, add onion and sauté until tender.
Add flour and blend until smooth. Add tomatoes, capsicum
and seasonings and stirring continuously, bring to the boil.
Cook 2-3 minutes.

Place rice in an even layer in the base of a greased ovenproof
casserole, arrange fillets of fish on top, sprinkle with lemon
juice. Cover with tomato mixture. Cook in a moderate oven
for 35-40 minutes or until fish is tender. Sprinkle with finely
chopped parsley and serve piping hot.

Tuna Savoury

Quick and easy.

Time: 30 minutes
Temperature: 375-400° F
Serves: 4

2 oz butter or margarine
4 tablespoons (2 oz) plain flour
1 cup milk
salt and pepper
1x12 oz can tuna
1x6 oz can evaporated milk
1x8 oz can condensed mushroom soup
1 cup peas, cooked
1 cup crushed potato crisps
¼ cup grated Cheddar cheese
1 cup fresh white breadcrumbs
extra 1 oz butter or margarine

Melt butter in a saucepan, add flour and stir until smooth, cook 1-2 minutes. Add milk and stirring continuously, bring to the boil, season to taste with salt and pepper.

Remove skin and bones from tuna and add to sauce with evaporated milk, mushroom soup, peas and potato crisps. Mix together thoroughly and place in a greased ovenproof casserole. Combine grated cheese and breadcrumbs and sprinkle on top, dot with butter.

Place in a moderately hot oven for approximately 30 minutes or until hot and golden brown on top. Serve with crusty French bread and a tossed green salad.

LUNCH AND SUPPER CASSEROLES

Here is a selection of casseroles especially
suitable for light lunches and suppers.
Eggs, poultry, fish and vegetables combine
to make new, tasty casseroles. All can be
prepared in advance. When a group of
friends call in for lunch or when the family
want to watch television by a roaring log
fire, these recipes will stand you in good
stead. They can be served straight from the
oven.

Cheese Pudding

Time: 20-30 minutes
Temperature: 400-450° F
Serves: 4

1 pint milk
2 cups soft white breadcrumbs
1 teaspoon dry mustard
½ teaspoon salt
freshly ground pepper
5 oz tasty cheese, grated
2 eggs, separated

Heat milk in a saucepan and pour over breadcrumbs, add seasonings, cheese and beaten egg yolks. Whip egg whites in a mixing bowl until stiff, fold gently into cheese mixture.

Pour into a greased ovenproof casserole and bake in a hot oven for 20-30 minutes until set. Serve immediately with a tossed green salad and sliced tomatoes seasoned with salt, pepper and sugar.

Cabbage Rolls

Time: approximately 1 hour
Temperature: 375-400° F
Serves: 4

½ oz butter or margarine
4 oz mushrooms, sliced
6 shallots, sliced
1 cup cooked rice
2 hard-boiled eggs, chopped
salt
freshly ground pepper
1 cabbage
1x16 oz can condensed tomato soup
finely chopped parsley for garnish

In a small saucepan, melt butter and sauté mushrooms and shallots lightly. Place mixture in a bowl and add rice and eggs and season to taste with salt and pepper.

Discard tough outer leaves of cabbage. Blanch whole cabbage in boiling salted water for 5-10 minutes, drain well. Carefully detach leaves and remove any hard stems with kitchen scissors. Select 8 leaves and place some filling on each. Roll up like a parcel, folding in the ends, secure with cocktail sticks. Arrange in an ovenproof casserole and pour over tomato soup. Cover and cook in a moderately hot oven for approximately 1 hour or until tender. Remove cocktail sticks and sprinkle with chopped parsley before serving.

Cauliflower Savoury

This delicious luncheon dish may also be served as a vegetable with grilled steaks.

Time: 20-30 minutes
Temperature: 375-400° F
Serves: 4

1 large cauliflower
6 rashers bacon
½ oz lard or dripping
1 onion, finely chopped

Cheese Sauce:
1½ oz butter or margarine
3 tablespoons (1½ oz) plain flour
¾ pint combined milk and cauliflower water
salt and pepper
4 oz Cheddar cheese, grated

Wash cauliflower and break into sprigs. Cook in boiling salted water for 8-10 minutes, or until just tender. Drain well and reserve water. Place cauliflower in a greased ovenproof casserole.

Remove rind from bacon and chop. Melt lard in a small saucepan and add bacon and onion, cook until onion is tender, sprinkle over cauliflower in casserole.

Pour cheese sauce over cauliflower and sprinkle reserved cheese on top. Cook in a moderately hot oven for 20-30 minutes or until hot and lightly browned on top.

Cheese Sauce: Melt butter in a small saucepan and blend in flour until smooth, cook for 1 minute. Add combined milk and cauliflower water and stirring continuously, bring to the boil. Simmer gently for 5 minutes and season to taste with salt and pepper. Remove from heat, add grated cheese (reserving 1 tablespoon for the top). Stir sauce until smooth.

Curried Eggs

Time: approximately 20 minutes
Temperature: 375-400° F
Serves: 4-6

6 hard-boiled eggs
¼ cup soft white breadcrumbs
½ oz butter or margarine
boiled rice for serving

Curry Sauce:
2 oz butter or margarine
1 cup sliced celery
1 onion, finely chopped
1-2 teaspoons curry powder (according to taste)
3 tablespoons (1½ oz) plain flour
2 cups milk
salt
freshly ground pepper

Cut eggs in halves lengthways, arrange in a greased shallow ovenproof casserole. Pour curry sauce over eggs, sprinkle with breadcrumbs and dot with butter. Cook in a moderately hot oven for approximately 20 minutes or until golden brown on top. Serve with boiled rice and a tossed green salad.

Curry Sauce: Melt butter in a saucepan and add celery, onion and curry powder, sauté until onion is tender and golden. Add flour and mix thoroughly. Add milk and stirring continuously, bring to boil. Season to taste with salt and pepper.

Egg and Potato Casserole

Time: 15-20 minutes
Temperature: 375-400° F
Serves: 4

1 lb potatoes
2 oz butter or margarine
6 hard-boiled eggs, chopped
1 teaspoon finely chopped chives
1 teaspoon finely chopped parsley
½ teaspoon French mustard
salt
freshly ground pepper
½ cup chopped ham
1 cup sour cream
2 tablespoons grated tasty cheese

Peel potatoes, cook until just tender in boiling salted water, slice thickly. Heat butter in a frying pan and fry potatoes until golden on both sides.

Arrange potato in a greased ovenproof casserole and cover with egg, chives, parsley, mustard, salt and pepper to taste and ham. Pour sour cream over and sprinkle with cheese.

Bake in a moderately hot oven for approximately 15-20 minutes or until hot and golden brown on top. Serve immediately.

Egg and Prawn Bake

Time: 20-30 minutes
Temperature: 350-375° F
Serves: 4

1 oz butter or margarine
2 tablespoons (1 oz) plain flour
1x10 oz can condensed mushroom soup
½ cup dry white wine
salt
freshly ground pepper
2 tablespoons finely chopped parsley
6 hard-boiled eggs, sliced
1 cup shelled prawns, cooked
½ cup soft white breadcrumbs
extra 1 oz butter or margarine
boiled rice for serving

Melt butter in a saucepan, add flour and blend until smooth. Add soup and wine and stirring continuously, bring to the boil. Season to taste with salt and pepper and add parsley.

Grease an ovenproof casserole and arrange half the eggs over the base, place prawns on top and cover with a second layer of egg. Pour sauce over, sprinkle with breadcrumbs and dot with butter.

Cook in a moderate oven for 20-30 minutes or until hot and golden brown on top. Serve with boiled rice.

Spanish Eggs

Time: 10-15 minutes
Temperature: 400-450° F
Serves: 6

1 tablespoon oil
1 onion, chopped
6 oz garlic sausage, chopped
1 green capsicum, seeded and chopped
2 lb tomatoes, skinned and chopped
1 teaspoon salt
freshly ground pepper
1 teaspoon sugar
½ pint water
2 tablespoons tomato paste
1x6 oz packet frozen peas
6 eggs

Heat oil in a saucepan, add onion and sauté until transparent
and soft. Add all remaining ingredients except eggs, mix well,
cover and simmer gently for 20 minutes. Remove lid from
saucepan and cook for a further 10 minutes to allow liquid to
reduce. Pour tomato mixture into a greased shallow ovenproof
casserole, level surface with a spatula.

Using the back of a serving spoon, make 6 hollows in the
mixture, break an egg into each. Bake in a hot oven, uncovered,
for 10-15 minutes or until eggs are set. Serve with hot crusty
French bread.

Scalloped Potatoes and Leeks

Time: approximately 2 hours
Temperature: 300-325° F
Serves: 4

1½-2 lb potatoes
3-4 rashers bacon
1 large onion, chopped
3 leeks, finely sliced
salt
freshly ground pepper
1 oz butter or margarine
chopped parsley for garnish

White Sauce:
¾ pint milk
½ bay leaf
2 sprigs parsley
1 oz butter or margarine
1 oz (2 tablespoons) plain flour
salt and pepper

Scrub and peel potatoes, cut into ¼-inch slices. Blanch in boiling salted water for 5 minutes, drain. Remove rind from bacon and cut into 1-inch pieces, fry until golden brown.

Grease an ovenproof casserole and alternate layers of potato, onion, leeks and bacon, season each layer with salt and pepper, dot with butter. Pour white sauce over ingredients in casserole. Cover and cook in a slow oven for approximately 2 hours. Sprinkle with chopped parsley. Serve with a tossed green salad.

White Sauce: Place milk, bay leaf and parsley in a saucepan, bring to simmering point, remove from heat and stand aside for 10 minutes. Strain milk.

Melt butter in a saucepan and blend in flour until smooth. Add milk and stirring continuously, bring to the boil. Season to taste with salt and pepper.

Ham and Asparagus Casserole

Time: 20-30 minutes
Temperature: 375-400° F
Serves: 4

2 stalks celery, sliced
1 oz butter or margarine
1 x 16 oz can asparagus soup
½ cup water
freshly ground pepper
1½ cups cooked rice
1 cup chopped ham
1 x 16 oz can asparagus pieces, drained
¼ cup grated Parmesan cheese

In a saucepan, sauté celery in butter until tender. Add asparagus soup, water and pepper.

Grease a shallow ovenproof casserole. Place rice in casserole and cover with a layer of chopped ham and asparagus pieces. Gently pour soup mixture over casserole and sprinkle cheese on top. Cook in a moderately hot oven for 20-30 minutes or until heated through. Serve with crusty French bread.

PRAWN CRÉOLE
(see page 108)

BAKED BEAN CASSEROLE
(see page 56)

Clobassy Sausage Casserole

Time: 20-30 minutes
Temperature: 350-375° F
Serves: 4

4 large potatoes
1-1½ lb clobassy sausage
salt
freshly ground pepper
1x10 oz carton sour cream

Cook potatoes in boiling salted water until tender, peel and slice. Remove skin from sausage and slice.

Grease an ovenproof casserole and alternate layers of potato, seasoned with salt and pepper and sliced sausage. Finish with a layer of potato. Pour sour cream over top.

Cook in a moderate oven for 20-30 minutes or until hot. Serve with crusty French bread.

Hawaiian Cutlets

Time: 30-45 minutes
Temperature: 350-375° F
Serves: 4

8 lamb cutlets
2 tablespoons (1 oz) seasoned flour
1 oz butter or margarine
juice of 3 oranges
½ cup stock or water and beef stock cube
2 tablespoons redcurrant jelly

Trim excess fat from cutlets and flatten. Dip in seasoned flour. Heat butter in a flameproof casserole and lightly brown cutlets remove from casserole. Place remaining ingredients in casserole and stirring continuously, bring to the boil.

Return cutlets to casserole, cover and cook in a moderate oven for 30-45 minutes or until cutlets are tender. Serve with buttered new potatoes and peas.

Chicken Supreme

Time: approximately 20 minutes
Temperature: 350-375° F
Serves: 4

1x3 lb chicken, cooked
1 large green capsicum
2 oz button mushrooms
1½ oz butter or margarine
2 tablespoons (1 oz) plain flour
1¼ cups chicken stock or water and chicken stock cubes
3 tablespoons cream
½ teaspoon salt
freshly ground pepper
crescents of puff pastry for garnish

Remove meat from chicken carcase and cut into bite-size pieces. Seed and slice capsicum, blanch in boiling salted water for 2-3 minutes, drain. Wipe mushrooms and cut into quarters, sauté in ½ oz of the butter for 2-3 minutes, stand aside.

Melt remaining butter in a flameproof casserole, add flour and blend until smooth, cook until golden. Add stock and stirring continuously, bring to the boil. Add cream and boil rapidly until of a syrupy consistency. Add seasonings, chicken, capsicum and mushrooms. Mix thoroughly, cover and cook in a moderate oven for approximately 20 minutes or until hot.

Before serving, garnish with crescents of puff pastry.

Chicken Tetrazzini

Time: 30-45 minutes
Temperature: 375-400° F
Serves: 4

3 oz butter or margarine
8 oz mushrooms, sliced
8 oz macaroni, cooked
4 tablespoons (2 oz) plain flour
1 pint chicken stock or water and chicken stock cubes
salt
freshly ground pepper
1 cup cream
2 tablespoons dry sherry
1 cup diced cooked chicken
¼ cup grated Parmesan cheese

Melt 1 oz of the butter in a saucepan and sauté mushrooms until tender, mix with macaroni. Melt remaining butter in a saucepan, add flour and blend until smooth. Add chicken stock and stirring continuously, bring to the boil. Season to taste with salt and pepper. Add cream and sherry, mix thoroughly. Mix half the sauce with combined mushrooms and macaroni and the other half with the chicken.

Grease an ovenproof casserole and place macaroni mixture in base. Make a well in the centre and add chicken. Sprinkle top of casserole with Parmesan cheese.

Cook in a moderately hot oven for 30-45 minutes or until hot and golden brown on top.

Variation: ½ cup blanched almonds may be added to chicken mixture.

Old Fashioned Fish Pie

Time: 30-35 minutes
Temperature: 375-400° F
    increasing to 400-450° F
Serves: 4

12 oz smoked cod
½ pint milk
2 hard-boiled eggs, sliced
1 oz butter or margarine
2 tablespoons (1 oz) plain flour
salt
freshly ground pepper
1 lb old potatoes
1 oz butter or margarine
2 tablespoons hot milk
extra salt and pepper
2 tablespoons grated Parmesan cheese

Place fish in a greased ovenproof casserole, add half the milk, cover and poach in a moderately hot oven for 10-15 minutes. Remove fish from casserole, drain and reserve milk. Bone and flake fish, replace in casserole with hard-boiled eggs.

In a saucepan, melt butter and blend in flour until smooth. Add remaining milk and milk from poached fish. Stirring continuously, bring to the boil. Season to taste with salt and pepper, pour over fish.

Peel potatoes and cook in boiling salted water until tender. Drain thoroughly and mash. Add butter, milk and extra salt and pepper to taste. Spread potato evenly over fish and sprinkle with Parmesan cheese.

Place casserole in a hot oven for approximately 20 minutes or until heated through and top is crisp and golden brown. Serve immediately.

Fish Valencia

An ideal luncheon dish or entrée.

Time: 30 minutes
Temperature: 350-375° F
Serves: 3-4

1 lb fish fillets (snapper or flathead)
salt and pepper
juice and grated rind of 1 lemon
3 shallots, finely chopped
2 large tomatoes, sliced
2 tablespoons fine dry breadcrumbs
4 tablespoons grated Cheddar cheese
1 oz butter or margarine

Cut fish into serving pieces and arrange in a greased ovenproof casserole. Season with salt, pepper and juice and rind of lemon. Cover with shallots, tomato, breadcrumbs, cheese and finally dot with butter.

Cover casserole and cook in a moderate oven for 15 minutes, remove lid and cook uncovered, for a further 15 minutes.

INSTANT CASSEROLES

Every housewife, at some stage, has to produce a meal quickly. Using instant seasonings, packet sauces and canned vegetables and meats, meals can be produced in minutes. The variety of convenience foods available in supermarkets today makes it possible to produce innumerable casseroles. A meal in one casserole which can be left to cook in the oven is a great boon to the housewife. They are ideal for busy households.

Baked Cheese Eggs

Bake in a large casserole or in individual ramekins.

Time: 15 minutes
Temperature: 350-375° F
Serves: 4

4 oz Cheddar cheese
1 oz butter or margarine
4 eggs
salt
freshly ground pepper
4 tablespoons cream or top of milk
hot buttered toast for serving

Grate 1 oz of the cheese and thinly slice remaining cheese.

Grease the base of a shallow ovenproof casserole with butter and cover with slices of cheese. Break eggs carefully on to cheese, making sure yolks do not break. Season with salt and pepper, pour a spoonful of cream on top of each egg and sprinkle with grated cheese.

Bake uncovered, in a moderate oven for 15 minutes or until eggs are set. Serve immediately with hot buttered toast.

Baked Bean Casserole

Time: approximately 15 minutes
Temperature: 350-375° F
Serves: 4

8 frankfurters
2 oz lard or dripping
1 large onion, chopped
1 small green capsicum, seeded and chopped
2x16 oz can baked beans in tomato sauce
salt
freshly ground pepper
grilled bacon for serving

Cut frankfurters into 2-inch lengths. Melt lard in a flameproof
casserole, sauté onion and capsicum until tender. Add baked
beans, frankfurters and seasonings to taste. Mix well, cover and
cook in a moderate oven for approximately 15 minutes or
until hot. Serve with grilled bacon.

Casserole of Potatoes

Time: 45 minutes - 1 hour
Temperature: 375-400° F
Serves: 4

1 clove garlic, crushed
1 lb potatoes, peeled
salt
freshly ground pepper
2 oz tasty cheese, grated
stock or water and chicken stock cube
1 oz butter or margarine

Grease an ovenproof casserole and spread garlic over base.
Slice potatoes and place in casserole, seasoning each layer
with salt, pepper and grated cheese.

Pour in enough stock to barely cover potatoes, dot with butter.
Cook in a moderately hot oven for 45 minutes - 1 hour or
until potatoes are tender and golden brown on top.

Tomato Casserole

Time: approximately 35 minutes
Temperature: 325-350° F
Serves: 4

6 oz macaroni
1 onion, chopped
8 oz tomatoes, skinned and sliced
2 oz Parmesan cheese, grated
grilled bacon rolls and chopped parsley for garnish

Ham and Cheese Sauce:
2 eggs
1 teaspoon French mustard
1 cup milk
½ oz butter or margarine, melted
2 oz ham, chopped
2 oz Cheddar cheese, grated
salt
pinch of cayenne pepper

Cook macaroni and onion in boiling salted water for approximately 12 minutes or until macaroni is just tender. Drain and rinse thoroughly. Place half the noodles in a greased ovenproof casserole, cover with tomatoes, place remaining noodles on top. Pour ham and cheese sauce gently over ingredients in casserole. Sprinkle with cheese.

Cook in a moderately slow oven for approximately 35 minutes or until mixture sets. Garnish with grilled bacon rolls and chopped parsley and serve piping hot.

Ham and Cheese Sauce: In a mixing bowl, combine eggs, mustard, milk, butter, ham, cheese and season to taste with salt and cayenne pepper. Beat together thoroughly.

Beef Stroganoff

Time: approximately 1 hour
Temperature: 350-375° F
Serves: 4

1½ lb lean round steak
salt and pepper
1 oz butter or margarine
2 onions, thinly sliced
1x8 oz can mushrooms in butter sauce
1x8 oz can reduced cream
2 tablespoons dry sherry

Cut steak into thin strips, 1½-inches long x ¼-inch wide,
season with salt and pepper. Heat butter in a flameproof
casserole and brown meat evenly. Remove from casserole
and sauté onions in remaining butter until golden brown.
Return meat to casserole and add mushrooms and cream.

Cover casserole and cook in a moderate oven for approximately
1 hour or until meat is tender. Add sherry just before serving.
Accompany with boiled rice and a green vegetable.

Farmhouse Stew

Time: approximately 1 hour
Temperature: 350-375° F
Serves: 4

1½ lb lean chuck steak
2 carrots, sliced
2 potatoes, diced
1 packet dehydrated vegetable soup
¾ pint stock or water and beef stock cube
1 tablespoon tomato sauce
salt
freshly ground pepper

Trim steak and cut into 1-inch pieces. Place meat and vegetables in an ovenproof casserole. Combine soup, stock, tomato sauce and seasonings and add to casserole.

Cover and cook in a moderate oven for approximately 1 hour or until meat is tender.

Instant Steak Casserole

Time: approximately 30 minutes
Temperature: 350-375° F
Serves: 4

1x16 oz can braized steak
1x10 oz packet frozen mixed vegetables, thawed
1 packet dehydrated French onion soup
1 tablespoon (½ oz) cornflour
¾ pint stock or water and beef stock cube
2 large potatoes, cooked and thinly sliced
2 tablespoons finely chopped parsley for garnish

Place steak in an ovenproof casserole and add vegetables.
Blend soup, cornflour and stock together, pour over ingredients
in casserole. Top with a layer of potatoes. Cook in a moderate
oven for approximately 30 minutes or until hot and potatoes
are lightly browned on top. Sprinkle with finely chopped
parsley before serving.

Swiss Mushroom Steak

Time: approximately 1 hour
Temperature: 350-375° F
Serves: 4

1½ lb lean blade steak
2 tablespoons dripping
1x10 oz can condensed mushroom soup
½ cup milk
salt
freshly ground pepper

Trim steak and cut into 1-inch pieces. Heat dripping in a
flameproof casserole and brown meat evenly. Add combined
soup and milk and season to taste with salt and pepper.

Cover and cook in a moderate oven for approximately 1 hour
or until meat is tender. Serve with boiled rice or new potatoes
tossed in butter and chopped parsley.

Mexican Chilli Casserole

Time: approximately 30 minutes
Temperature: 350-375° F
Serves: 4

1 tablespoon oil
1 lb minced steak
2 onions, finely chopped
1x5 oz can tomato paste
¾ cup water
1 packet chilli seasoning mix
1x10 oz can butter beans, drained
12 stuffed olives, sliced
3 oz tasty cheese, grated

Heat oil in a frying pan, cook meat until lightly browned. Add onion, tomato paste, water and chilli seasoning mix. Mix together thoroughly and simmer for 10 minutes.

In a greased ovenproof casserole, alternate layers of meat mixture, beans, olives and cheese, finish with a sprinkling of cheese. Cook in a moderate oven for approximately 30 minutes or until hot.

Quick Italian Spaghetti

Time: approximately 20 minutes
Temperature: 350-375° F
Serves: 4

2 tablespoons olive oil
2 green capsicums, seeded and chopped
1 clove garlic, crushed
3 onions, sliced
1 lb minced steak
1 tablespoon Worcestershire sauce
1x14 oz can peeled tomatoes
salt
freshly ground pepper
1x12 oz packet spaghetti
grated Parmesan cheese for serving

Heat oil in a frying pan, sauté capsicum, garlic and onion until tender and onion is golden brown. Add steak and cook until meat changes colour, add Worcestershire sauce, tomatoes and salt and pepper to taste. Mix together thoroughly.

Meanwhile, cook spaghetti in boiling salted water until just tender, drain and rinse thoroughly. Grease an ovenproof casserole and place spaghetti in casserole, cover with sauce. Cover and cook in a moderate oven for approximately 20 minutes or until hot. Top each serving with grated Parmesan cheese.

Apple and Meat Loaf

Served hot with vegetables or cold with salad, this is delicious.

Time: approximately 1¼ hours
Temperature: 325-350° F
Serves: 6

2 cooking apples
1½ lb minced steak
1½ cups soft white breadcrumbs
1 onion, finely chopped
salt
freshly ground pepper
1 teaspoon Worcestershire sauce
2 eggs
3 tablespoons tomato sauce
2 tablespoons (1 oz) brown sugar

Peel, core and grate apples. Combine grated apple, minced steak, breadcrumbs, onion, seasonings to taste and Worcestershire sauce in a large mixing bowl. Beat eggs and add, mix thoroughly.

Press mixture into a greased ovenproof casserole, level surface with a spatula. Spoon tomato sauce over top and sprinkle with brown sugar. Cook in a moderately slow oven for approximately 1¼ hours or until cooked. Baste occasionally with dripping which collects around the sides of the casserole.

Pour off excess fat and serve hot or cold, cut into slices.

Veal with Pineapple

Time: 1¼ hours
Temperature: 350-375° F
Serves: 6

6 veal chops or cutlets
4 tablespoons (2 oz) seasoned flour
2 oz butter or margarine
¾ cup pineapple juice
2 tablespoons lemon juice
1 tablespoon Worcestershire sauce
6 slices pineapple
boiled rice for serving

Coat chops with seasoned flour. Heat 1 oz of the butter in a flameproof casserole and brown chops evenly on both sides. Add pineapple juice, lemon juice and Worcestershire sauce, cover and cook gently in a moderate oven for approximately 1¼ hours or until chops are tender.

Meanwhile, dip pineapple in seasoned flour and fry in remaining butter until lightly brown on both sides. To serve, place a slice of pineapple on top of each chop and accompany with boiled rice.

QUICK ITALIAN SPAGHETTI
(see page 62)

OXTAIL RAGOÛT
(see page 96)

Ham and Cheese Rolls

Time: approximately 30 minutes
Temperature: 350-375° F
Serves: 4

8 slices pressed shoulder ham
French mustard
8 slices processed Cheddar cheese
1x16 oz can condensed celery soup
¼ cup water
boiled rice or hot French bread for serving

Spread ham thinly with French mustard and place a slice of cheese on top. Roll up and secure with cocktail sticks.

Place in a single layer in a shallow greased ovenproof casserole. Mix soup and water together and pour over ham rolls. Cover casserole and cook in a moderate oven for approximately 30 minutes or until hot.

Serve with boiled rice or hot French bread.

Macaroni Special

Time: approximately 45 minutes
Temperature: 300-325° F
Serves: 4

2 oz butter or margarine
1 onion, thinly sliced
1 clove garlic, crushed
1x7¾ oz can mushrooms in butter sauce
1x15 oz can peeled tomatoes
1x5 oz can tomato paste
8 oz macaroni, cooked
8 oz ham, finely chopped
4 tablespoons dry white wine or sherry
1 teaspoon sugar
salt
freshly ground pepper
grated Parmesan cheese and finely chopped parsley for garnish

Melt butter in a flameproof casserole, sauté onion and garlic until tender. Add all remaining ingredients except Parmesan cheese and parsley and mix together thoroughly. Cover and cook in a slow oven for approximately 45 minutes or until hot.

Sprinkle with Parmesan cheese and parsley and serve with hot crusty French bread.

Pork Chops in Sour Cream

Time: 1 hour
Temperature: 350-375° F
Serves: 4

4 pork loin chops, ½-inch thick
2 tablespoons (1 oz) seasoned flour
4 whole cloves
1 oz butter or margarine
½ cup water
½ bay leaf
2 tablespoons vinegar
1 tablespoon (½ oz) sugar
½ cup sour cream
salt
freshly ground pepper

Coat chops with seasoned flour. Insert one clove in each chop. Heat butter in a flameproof casserole and brown chops lightly on both sides.

Combine remaining ingredients and pour over chops. Cover casserole and cook in a moderate oven for 1 hour or until chops are tender. Serve with a green vegetable.

Pork Provençale

Time: 1-1¼ hours
Temperature: 375-400° F
  reducing to 350-375° F
Serves: 4

4 pork chump chops
2 tablespoons (1 oz) seasoned flour
1 oz butter or margarine
½ cup finely chopped onion
1 clove garlic, crushed
4 large tomatoes, thickly sliced
salt and pepper
pinch of sugar
green olives and finely chopped parsley for garnish

Trim excess fat from chops, dip in seasoned flour. Heat butter in a flameproof casserole and cook onion and garlic until golden brown, drain and remove from casserole. Brown chops evenly on both sides in remaining butter. Add cooked onion to chops and cover with tomatoes. Season to taste with salt, pepper and sugar.

Cover casserole and cook in moderately hot oven for 30 minutes. Reduce oven temperature to moderate and cook for a further 30-45 minutes, or until meat is tender. Garnish with olives and parsley before serving.

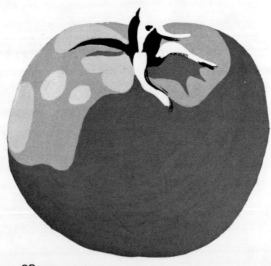

Frankfurter Casserole

A favourite with children.

Time: 15-20 minutes
Temperature: 350-375° F
Serves: 4

½ oz butter or margarine
½ cup finely sliced celery
1 large onion, finely chopped
1x16 oz can condensed tomato soup
1 teaspoon Worcestershire sauce
1 teaspoon French mustard
salt and pepper
1½ lb frankfurters
8 oz spaghetti or noodles

Heat butter in a frying pan, sauté celery and onion until
golden. Add tomato soup, Worcestershire sauce, mustard
and salt and pepper to taste. Bring to the boil, mixing
thoroughly.

Slice frankfurters diagonally into 1-inch pieces, add to sauce.

Meanwhile, cook spaghetti in boiling salted water until tender,
drain and rinse thoroughly. Place spaghetti in a greased
ovenproof casserole, pour sauce over. Cook in a moderate
oven for 15-20 minutes or until hot.

Quick Chicken Dish

Time: approximately 1 hour
Temperature: 325-350° F
Serves: 4

1 oz butter or margarine
4 chicken portions
1x16 oz can condensed chicken soup
¼ cup dry sherry
¼ cup grated Cheddar cheese (optional)
boiled rice or hot crusty French bread for serving

Heat butter in a flameproof casserole, cook chicken pieces
until golden brown. Mix chicken soup and sherry together,
pour over chicken pieces, sprinkle with grated cheese if
desired.

Cover casserole and cook in a moderately slow oven for
approximately 1 hour or until chicken is tender. Remove
lid from casserole for last 15 minutes of cooking time. Serve
with boiled rice or hot crusty French bread.

Turkey Casserole

Time: approximately 30 minutes
Temperature: 300-325° F
Serves: 6-8

1 packet stroganoff sauce mix
1½ cups water
½ cup sour cream
4 cups diced cooked turkey
8 oz macaroni, cooked
1x10 oz packet frozen peas, cooked
2 oz green olives, stoned and sliced
2 tablespoons soft white breadcrumbs
2 tablespoons slivered blanched almonds
1 oz butter

Place stroganoff sauce mix in a saucepan and stirring
continuously, blend in water. Bring to the boil, cover and
simmer gently for 10 minutes. Add sour cream and turkey
and mix thoroughly.

Grease an ovenproof casserole and alternate layers of
macaroni, peas, turkey mixture and olives. Sprinkle top of
casserole with breadcrumbs and almonds and dot with butter.
Cook in a slow oven for approximately 30 minutes or until
hot.

Note: Chicken may be used instead of turkey.

Botany Bay Bake

Time: 30 minutes
Temperature: 350-375° F
Serves: 4

2 oz butter or margarine
1 onion, thinly sliced
½ capsicum, seeded and finely chopped
salt
freshly ground pepper
pinch each of dried sage and thyme
1 bay leaf
1½ lb fillets of snapper
4 tomatoes, skinned and sliced
4 rashers bacon
½ cup dry white wine

Melt butter in a flameproof casserole, sauté onion and
capsicum until tender. Add seasonings, herbs and bay leaf,
mix together.

Place fillets of fish on top of vegetables and cover with
tomato. Remove rind from bacon, cut rashers in halves
and place on top of tomatoes. Add wine to casserole.

Bake fish, uncovered, in a moderate oven for 30 minutes or
until cooked. Serve with creamed potato and a green
vegetable.

ECONOMICAL CASSEROLES

Housewives often have problems stretching the family budget. Casseroles are ideal for using cheaper cuts of meat that will become succulent and tender with slow, gentle cooking in the oven. A little meat, poultry or cooked vegetables go a long way when combined with tasty sauces and gravies. Combined with pasta, they are also delicious. Left-overs can be transformed into completely new meals. Casserole cookery is especially economical and nutritious because vegetable and meat juices are retained.

Brain and Tomato Casserole

Time: 30-35 minutes
Temperature: 350-375° F
Serves: 4

4 sets lambs' brains
1 lb tomatoes, skinned and sliced
1 onion, chopped
4 rashers bacon, de-rinded and cut into 1-inch pieces
salt
freshly ground pepper
1 tablespoon finely chopped parsley
2 eggs
1 cup milk
1 cup soft white breadcrumbs
½ oz butter or margarine
grilled bacon rolls and parsley sprigs for garnish

Soak brains for 30 minutes in salted water, drain. Remove skin and membrane. Cover with cold water, bring to the boil, drain and cut into bite-size pieces.

Alternate layers of tomato, onion, brains and bacon in a greased ovenproof casserole. Season each layer with salt, pepper and chopped parsley.

Combine eggs and milk, beat well, pour gently over ingredients in casserole. Sprinkle breadcrumbs over top of casserole and dot with butter. Cook in a moderate oven for 30-35 minutes or until mixture is set and golden brown on top. Garnish with bacon rolls and parsley sprigs before serving.

Sweet Curry

Time: 55 minutes
Serves: 4

1 cooking apple
1 tomato
1 banana
1 onion, chopped
½ oz butter or margarine
1-2 tablespoons curry powder, according to taste
1 tablespoon (½ oz) plain flour
¾ pint stock or water and beef stock cube
1 tablespoon desiccated coconut
2 oz sultanas
2 tablespoons jam or chutney
juice of ½ lemon
salt
freshly ground pepper
1 lb cold cooked meat
boiled rice for serving

Peel, core and slice apple, skin and slice tomato and banana.

In a flameproof casserole, fry onion in butter until golden
brown. Add prepared apple, tomato, banana, curry powder
and flour, mix together thoroughly and fry for 5 minutes.
Add stock and stirring continuously, bring to the boil. Add
coconut, sultanas, jam and lemon juice and season to taste
with salt and pepper. Cover and simmer over a gentle heat
for approximately 45 minutes

Meanwhile, remove all fat and gristle from meat and cut into
½-inch pieces. Add to curry sauce, mix thoroughly, cover and
simmer for a further 10 minutes or until meat is hot. Do not
allow curry to boil once meat has been added as it will become
tough. Serve with boiled rice.

Lamb's Fry and Bacon

Equally good for breakfast, lunch or dinner.

Time: approximately 15 minutes
Serves: 4

1 lamb's fry
2 tablespoons (1 oz) seasoned flour
4 rashers bacon
1 oz butter or margarine
½ pint stock or water and beef stock cube
1 teaspoon lemon juice

Wash lamb's fry in cold salted water and remove skin and any tubes. Cut into thin slices and dip in seasoned flour. Remove rind from bacon and cut rashers in halves, fry in a flameproof casserole until golden brown, set aside.

Add butter to casserole and when hot, fry lamb's fry quickly on both sides, set aside. Add any remaining seasoned flour to casserole, blend until smooth. Add stock and lemon juice and stirring continuously, bring to the boil, adjust seasoning if necessary. Return lamb's fry and bacon to casserole, cover and simmer gently over a low heat for approximately 15 minutes or until tender.

Kidney and Bacon Rolls

Time: 30-35 minutes
Temperature: 375-400° F
   reducing to 350-375° F
Serves: 4

8 lambs' kidneys
4 rashers bacon
freshly ground pepper
4 tablespoons dry sherry or water

Soak kidneys in cold salted water for 30 minutes, remove skin and white core. Remove rind from bacon and cut each rasher in half. Wrap each kidney in a piece of bacon, secure with cocktail sticks.

Place in an ovenproof casserole, season with pepper and add sherry. Cover and cook in a moderately hot oven for 10 minutes. Reduce oven temperature to moderate and cook for a further 20-25 minutes, or until kidneys are tender. Remove cocktail sticks. Serve with vegetables as a dinner or on hot buttered toast for a luncheon or supper dish.

Piquant Chops

A quick casserole to make on a busy day.

Time: approximately 1½ hours
Temperature: 350-375° F
   reducing to 325-350° F
Serves: 4

4 mutton forequarter chops
1 small onion, chopped
1 clove garlic, crushed
1 tablespoon finely chopped green capsicum
1 tablespoon (½ oz) brown sugar
1 tablespoon curry powder
2 tablespoons Worcestershire sauce
2 tablespoons white vinegar
1 teaspoon French mustard
1x8 oz can condensed tomato soup
¼ cup stock or water and beef stock cube
salt
freshly ground pepper

Trim excess fat from chops, place in a greased ovenproof casserole. Add remaining ingredients, cover and marinate for 2-3 hours.

Cook in a moderate oven for approximately 30 minutes, reduce oven temperature to moderately slow and cook for a further 1 hour or until chops are tender. Serve with creamed potato and a green vegetable.

Spaghetti Chop Dinner

An ideal casserole for the family on a cold winter day.

Time: 1½ hours
Temperature: 350-375° F
  reducing to 325-350° F
Serves: 4

2 cups tomato juice
1 tablespoon (½ oz) brown sugar
1 teaspoon salt
freshly ground pepper
1 teaspoon dry mustard
2 tablespoons vinegar
1 tablespoon Worcestershire sauce
1 clove garlic, crushed
4 mutton forequarter chops
8 oz spaghetti, cooked
4 oz Cheddar cheese, grated

Combine tomato juice, sugar, salt and pepper, mustard, vinegar, Worcestershire sauce and garlic in a saucepan. Bring to the boil, cover and simmer gently for 10 minutes.

Meanwhile, brown chops on both sides under a hot grill.

In a greased ovenproof casserole, layer spaghetti, cheese and chops. Pour sauce over. Cover casserole and cook in a moderate oven for 30 minutes. Reduce temperature to moderately slow and cook for a further 1 hour or until chops are tender."

Lamb Shanks in Barbecue Sauce

Time: approximately 2 hours
Temperature: 300-325° F
Serves: 4

4 lamb shanks
2 rashers bacon
1 oz butter or margarine
1 onion, sliced
2 tablespoons (1 oz) plain flour
1x5 oz can tomato paste
1½ cups stock or water and beef stock cube
1 teaspoon salt
1 tablespoon (½ oz) brown sugar
1 tablespoon Worcestershire sauce
½ cup vinegar
1 teaspoon dry mustard

Wipe lamb shanks with a damp cloth. Remove rind from bacon and chop. Heat butter in a flameproof casserole, add onion and bacon and sauté until golden brown, remove from casserole. Dip lamb shanks in flour and brown evenly all over in remaining fat in casserole. Return onion and bacon to casserole, add remaining ingredients, bring to the boil and adjust seasonings if necessary.

Cover casserole and simmer gently in a slow oven for approximately 2 hours or until lamb shanks are tender. Serve with a green vegetable and creamed potatoes.

INGREDIENTS FOR INSTANT STEAK CASSEROLE
(see page 60)

BAKED CHEESE EGGS
(see page 55)

Creamed Tripe

Time: approximately 20 minutes
Temperature: 325-350° F
Serves: 4

1½ lb tripe, cooked
1 cup diced carrot, cooked
1 cup peas, cooked
2 tablespoons finely chopped parsley
½ cup soft white breadcrumbs
½ oz butter or margarine

White Sauce:
2 oz butter or margarine
1 onion, finely chopped
2 tablespoons (1 oz) plain flour
2 cups milk
salt
freshly ground pepper

Cut tripe into 1-inch pieces.

Mix tripe, carrot, peas, parsley and white sauce together.
Place in a greased ovenproof casserole, sprinkle with
breadcrumbs and dot with butter. Cook in a moderately
slow oven for approximately 20 minutes or until hot and
golden brown on top.

White Sauce: Melt butter in a saucepan, saute onion until
tender and transparent. Blend in flour and cook 1-2 minutes.
Add milk and stirring continuously, bring to the boil.
Season to taste with salt and pepper.

Pork Sausages and Apple

Time: 45 minutes - 1 hour
Temperature: 350-375° F
Serves: 4

1 oz butter or margarine
1½ lb pork sausages
1 onion, chopped
2 cooking apples
salt
freshly ground pepper
½ teaspoon ground ginger
2 tablespoons (1 oz) brown sugar
2 tablespoons (1 oz) plain flour
½ pint stock or water and beef stock cube
extra salt and pepper
creamed potato for serving

Heat butter in a frying pan, brown sausages evenly all over, remove from heat and drain on absorbent paper. Fry onion in remaining butter until golden brown, drain and set aside. Peel, core and slice apples.

Place sausages, onion and apple in layers in a greased ovenproof casserole, seasoning each layer with salt, pepper, ginger and sugar.

Add flour to remaining butter in frying pan, blend until smooth, cook 3-4 minutes or until nut brown. Add stock and stirring continuously, bring to the boil. Season to taste with extra salt and pepper. Pour gravy over ingredients in casserole and cook in a moderate oven for 45 minutes - 1 hour. Serve with creamed potato.

Sausages with Bacon and Cheese

Time: 20 minutes
Serves: 3-4

1 lb thick pork sausages
4 oz Cheddar cheese, sliced
6 rashers bacon
3 tablespoons fruit chutney
1x16 oz can condensed tomato soup
¼ cup water

Grill or fry sausages until golden brown. Slit sausages
lengthways, almost through. Place slices of cheese in the
sausages and press together again. Remove rind from bacon
and spread one side with chutney. Wrap around sausages
and secure with cocktail sticks.

In a flameproof casserole, cook bacon-wrapped sausages until
bacon is golden brown, pour off drippings. Mix soup and
water together and pour over casserole. Cover and simmer
gently for 20 minutes or until hot. Serve with baked jacket
potatoes.

Braised Cabbage with Apple

Time: approximately 30 minutes
Serves: 4

1 rasher bacon
1 tablespoon olive oil
1 small onion, chopped
2 tablespoons (1 oz) sugar
4 cups finely shredded cabbage
1 cooking apple, peeled, cored and sliced
1-2 tablespoons vinegar
3 tablespoons water
pinch of freshly grated nutmeg
salt and pepper
½ teaspoon caraway seeds (optional)

Remove rind from bacon and chop. Heat olive oil in a flameproof casserole, add bacon, onion and 1 tablespoon of the sugar. Stirring continuously, cook until golden brown. Add remaining ingredients and cover casserole.

Cook over a gentle heat for approximately 30 minutes or until cabbage is tender. Adjust seasonings if necessary and serve with grilled steak, chops, sausages or frankfurters.

Stuffed Green Capsicums

Time: 30-40 minutes
Temperature: 350-375° F
Serves: 6

6 large green capsicums
2 tablespoons olive oil
1 large onion, finely chopped
1 clove garlic, crushed
2 lb minced steak
1 teaspoon paprika pepper
salt
freshly ground pepper
4 tablespoons tomato paste
1 bay leaf
1 bacon stock cube
1½ cups hot water
2 tablespoons finely chopped parsley
1x8 oz carton cottage cheese
6 tablespoons grated tasty cheese

Cut tops off capsicums, remove seeds and membrane inside.
Heat oil in a saucepan and sauté onion and garlic until golden.
Add steak and cook until evenly brown. Add paprika pepper,
salt and pepper, 2 tablespoons of the tomato paste, bay leaf
and stock cube dissolved in 1 cup of the hot water. Cover
saucepan and simmer gently for 45 minutes. Remove bay leaf,
add parsley and adjust seasonings if necessary.

Meanwhile, blanch capsicums in a large saucepan of boiling
salted water. Drain and rinse well with cold water, dry
thoroughly. Place half the meat mixture into the capsicums,
divide cottage cheese into 6 portions and place on top, cover
with remaining meat mixture. Sprinkle grated cheese on top.

Place capsicums in a greased ovenproof casserole. Mix
remaining tomato paste with remaining water and pour
around capsicums. Bake in a moderate oven for 30-40 minutes
or until capsicums are tender, baste occasionally while
cooking.

Corn Casserole

Time: 20-25 minutes
Temperature: 350-375° F
Serves: 4

8 oz bacon rashers
1 cup fine dry breadcrumbs
1 onion, finely chopped
1 small green capsicum, seeded and chopped
1x16 oz can cream style sweet corn

Remove rind from bacon and chop into pieces. Cook slowly in a frying pan until golden brown but not crisp. Place breadcrumbs in a mixing bowl and pour drippings from bacon over, mix together. Add onion and capsicum to bacon in pan, cook slowly for a further 5 minutes, add sweet corn and mix together.

Alternate layers of sweet corn mixture and breadcrumbs in a greased ovenproof casserole, finishing with a layer of breadcrumbs.

Cook in a moderate oven for 20-25 minutes or until golden brown on top. Serve with grilled sausages.

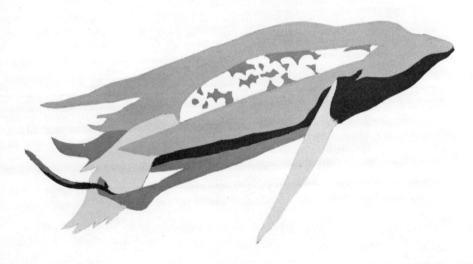

Macaroni Casserole

Time: 30-35 minutes
Temperature: 350-375° F
Serves: 4

2 tablespoons vegetable oil
2 onions, sliced
1 lb minced steak
1x15 oz can tomato purée
salt
freshly ground pepper
pinch of sugar
1 lb macaroni, cooked
4 oz Cheddar cheese, grated

Cheese Sauce:
1 oz butter or margarine
2 tablespoons (1 oz) plain flour
1 pint milk
3 eggs
4 oz Cheddar cheese, grated
salt and pepper

Heat oil in a frying pan, fry onion and meat until lightly browned. Add tomato purée and season to taste with salt, pepper and sugar, simmer gently for 20 minutes, stir occasionally.

Place half the macaroni in a greased ovenproof casserole, sprinkle with half the cheese, cover with meat mixture. Add remaining macaroni and pour over the cheese sauce. Sprinkle remaining cheese on top, cook in a moderate oven for 30-35 minutes or until mixture is set. Serve hot or cold, cut into slices. Serve with a tossed green salad.

Cheese Sauce: Melt butter in a saucepan and blend in flour until smooth. Add milk and stirring continuously, bring to the boil. Remove from heat and add beaten eggs one at a time. Return to gentle heat and add cheese, stir until melted. Season to taste with salt and pepper.

Cheese Potato Pie

A delicious luncheon dish.

Time: approximately 30 minutes
Temperature: 375-400° F
Serves: 4

1½ cups cold mashed potato
2 tablespoons (1 oz) plain flour
salt
freshly ground pepper
4 eggs
¾ pint sour cream
½ cup grated Cheddar cheese
grilled bacon for serving

Grease a deep ovenproof casserole.

Combine potato and flour and season to taste with salt and pepper.

In a mixing bowl, beat egg yolks and sour cream together, add grated cheese, reserving 2 tablespoons for the top. Mix potato with sour cream mixture. Whip egg whites until stiff and fold in gently.

Pour mixture into prepared ovenproof casserole and sprinkle top with reserved cheese. Bake in a moderately hot oven for approximately 30 minutes, or until golden brown on top. Serve immediately with grilled bacon.

Risotto

Time: 12-15 minutes
Serves: 3-4

1½ oz butter or margarine
1 onion, finely chopped
6 oz rice
4 oz mushrooms, sliced
1 clove garlic, crushed
1 bay leaf
salt and pepper
2 cups chicken stock or water and chicken stock cubes
1 oz tasty cheese, grated

Melt butter in a flameproof casserole, cook onion until golden.
Add unwashed rice and stirring continuously, cook for 1
minute. Add mushrooms, garlic, bay leaf, seasonings and half
the stock. Simmer gently, uncovered, for 12-15 minutes until
rice is just tender, add remaining stock as required. Remove
bay leaf, adjust seasonings if necessary.

Sprinkle with cheese, cover and stand in a warm place for 5
minutes. Mix Risotto lightly with a fork and serve immediately.

Tomato Bake

Time: 1-1½ hours
Temperature: 300-325° F
Serves: 4

½ cup fine dry breadcrumbs
4 large tomatoes, sliced
2 large cooking apples, peeled, cored and sliced
2 onions, finely sliced
salt
freshly ground pepper
1 tablespoon finely chopped mixed fresh herbs
1 oz butter or margarine

Grease an ovenproof casserole and sprinkle with half the breadcrumbs. Alternate layers of tomato, apple and onion in casserole, lightly seasoning each layer with salt, pepper and herbs. Sprinkle remaining breadcrumbs on top and dot with butter.

Cook in a slow oven for 1-1½ hours or until apples and onion are tender. Serve with grilled steaks, chops or sausages.

GOURMET CASSEROLES

Casseroles full of marvellous flavours and delicious aromas are meals that will please the most particular gourmet. Wine, eggs, cream, cheese—all go to enrich these tasty dishes. Cook them for both your family and friends.

Beef with Apricots

Time: approximately 2¼ hours
Temperature: 350-375° F
Serves: 6-8

¾ cup dried apricots
1 cup water
1 tablespoon vegetable oil
1x4 lb corner piece topside steak
1 cup finely chopped celery
1 onion, sliced
grated rind of 2 lemons
salt
freshly ground black pepper
2 teaspoons cornflour blended with 2 tablespoons water

Soak apricots in water overnight.

Heat oil in a deep flameproof casserole and brown meat evenly on all sides. Add all remaining ingredients except apricots and blended cornflour. Cover and cook in a moderate oven for approximately 2 hours or until meat is tender. Add soaked apricots and cook for a further 15 minutes.

Remove meat from casserole, carve and place on a serving plate. Garnish with apricots and keep in a warm place.

Thicken gravy with blended cornflour, adjust seasoning if necessary. Simmer for 5 minutes and serve with beef.

Beef with Olives

Time: 1¾-2¼ hours
Temperature: 350-375° F
Serves: 4

2 lb rump steak
2 tablespoons olive oil
1 oz butter or margarine
¼ cup brandy
¾ cup red wine
1 piece orange peel
1 clove garlic, crushed
bouquet garni
salt
freshly ground pepper
½ cup black olives, stoned
boiled rice for serving

Cut meat into 1-inch pieces. Heat olive oil and butter in a
flameproof casserole, brown meat evenly on all sides. Warm
brandy and pour over meat, ignite. Add red wine to casserole
and allow to boil for 30 seconds. Add all remaining ingredients
except olives.

Cover casserole and cook in a moderate oven for 1½-2 hours
or until meat is tender.

Remove bouquet garni, add olives and adjust seasonings if
necessary. Reheat for 15 minutes. Serve with boiled rice.

Ragoūt of Beef

Time: 1½-2 hours
Temperature: 350-375° F
Serves: 4

1½-2 lb topside steak
2 tablespoons dripping or bacon fat
8 small onions
1 tablespoon (½ oz) plain flour
½ cup red wine
3 cups beef stock or water and beef stock cubes
bouquet garni
1 clove garlic, crushed
salt and pepper
3-4 stalks celery
1 oz butter or margarine
2 oz walnut halves
extra ½ teaspoon salt
rind of 1 orange, finely shredded and blanched for garnish

Cut steak into 2-inch pieces. Heat dripping in a flameproof
casserole, add meat and fry until golden brown. Remove from
casserole, add onions and sauté until golden brown. Pour all
but 1 tablespoon of fat from casserole, add flour, blend
together and cook for a few minutes. Stirring continuously,
add wine and stock, bring to the boil. Add meat, bouquet
garni, garlic and salt and pepper to taste. Cover casserole and
cook in a moderate oven for 1½-2 hours or until meat is
tender.

Meanwhile, slice celery crossways. Heat butter in a frying pan
and sauté celery and walnuts with extra salt until crisp and
lightly brown. Add to casserole, adjust seasoning if necessary
and garnish with orange rind.

Serve with boiled rice or buttered new potatoes.

Steak with Orange Dumplings

Time: 1¾-2 hours
Temperature: 350-375° F
Serves: 5-6

1½ lb blade or skirt steak
1 tablespoon (½ oz) plain flour
salt
freshly ground pepper
1 teaspoon dry mustard
1 teaspoon brown sugar
2 tablespoons tomato sauce
1 teaspoon Worcestershire sauce
2 cups stock or water and beef stock cubes
1 onion, finely chopped
1 tablespoon finely chopped parsley

Orange Dumplings:
¾ cup (3 oz) self-raising flour
½ teaspoon salt
1½ oz suet, grated
1 tablespoon grated orange rind
combined orange juice and water to mix

Cut meat into 1-inch pieces. Combine, flour, salt, pepper, mustard and sugar and coat meat. Place in an ovenproof casserole.

Combine remaining ingredients and pour over meat. Cover casserole and cook in a moderate oven for 1 hour. Place dumplings on top of meat in casserole, cover and cook for a further 45 minutes - 1 hour.

Orange Dumplings: Sieve flour and salt into a mixing bowl, rub in suet. Add orange rind and mix to a soft dough with combined orange juice and water. Divide into small portions and roll into balls.

Oxtail Ragoût

Make a day in advance, the flavour is far better when reheated.

Time: 3½ hours
Temperature: 350-375° F
   reducing to 325-350° F
Serves: 3-4

1 oxtail, cut into joints
seasoned flour
3 tablespoons bacon fat
2 large onions, chopped
1 bay leaf
pinch of dried thyme
1x15 oz can tomatoes
2 beef stock cubes
1 cup red wine
1 stalk celery, sliced
2-3 leeks, sliced
1 parsnip, sliced
1 carrot, sliced
4 oz button mushrooms, sautéed in 1 oz butter or margarine
1 teaspoon salt
freshly ground pepper

Place oxtail in a large bowl, pour boiling water over and stand for 10 minutes, drain and wipe dry with absorbent paper.

Dip oxtail in seasoned flour. Heat bacon fat in a large flame-proof casserole, brown oxtail evenly on all sides and remove. Add onion to casserole and sauté until golden brown. Return oxtail to casserole and add bay leaf, thyme, tomatoes, stock cubes and red wine.

Cover casserole and simmer gently in a moderate oven for 1 hour, lower oven temperature to moderately slow and cook for a further 2 hours. Add prepared celery, leeks, parsnip and carrot and simmer for a further 30 minutes. Add mushrooms and season to taste with salt and pepper. When cool, place in refrigerator to chill overnight.

Next day, remove fat from surface and reheat in a moderate oven. Serve with baked jacket potatoes or hot crusty bread.

INGREDIENTS FOR STUFFED GREEN CAPSICUMS
(see page 85)

HAM AND ASPARAGUS CASSEROLE
(see page 48)

Beef and Pork Stew

Time: 2-2½ hours
Temperature: 350-375° F
Serves: 8-10

4 carrots, cut into 3-4 pieces
2 leeks, sliced
2 large onions, sliced
1 small green capsicum, seeded and chopped
1 small stalk celery, sliced
2½ lb brisket of beef
2 lb lean pickled pork
salt
freshly ground pepper
pinch of dried tarragon
pinch of dried thyme
1 tablespoon chopped parsley
1 bay leaf
3-4 cups beef stock or water and beef stock cubes
8 oz shelled peas

Place half the prepared vegetables in a large flameproof casserole. Place meat on top and cover with remaining vegetables. Add seasonings, herbs and enough stock to come half way up sides of meat. Cover casserole and bring to the boil.

Place casserole in a moderate oven and cook for 1½-2 hours. Add peas and cook for a further 30 minutes or until meat is tender.

Carve meat and serve with vegetables and gravy.

Veal with Mozzarella

Time: 30-35 minutes
Temperature: 350-375° F
Serves: 4-5

1½ lb veal steak, thinly cut
seasoned flour
1 egg beaten with ¼ cup water
1 cup fine dry breadcrumbs mixed with ¼ cup grated
  Parmesan cheese
oil for frying
extra 2 tablespoons oil
2 cloves garlic, crushed
1 onion, finely chopped
1x15 oz can peeled tomatoes
3 tablespoons tomato paste
¼ teaspoon dried thyme
½ teaspoon sugar
salt
freshly ground pepper
8 oz mozzarella cheese, thinly sliced

Trim meat and cut into serving-size pieces, flatten lightly. Dip
in seasoned flour, then in combined egg and water and finally
coat with combined breadcrumbs and Parmesan cheese. Press
crumbs on firmly.

Heat oil in a frying pan, fry veal until golden brown on both
sides. Drain on absorbent paper.

Heat extra oil in a saucepan, add garlic and onion and sauté
5 minutes. Add tomatoes, tomato paste, thyme, sugar and salt
and pepper to taste, cover, simmer 10 minutes.

Pour one-third of tomato mixture into an ovenproof casserole,
arrange veal on top, cover with cheese and pour over remaining
sauce. Cook, uncovered, in a moderate oven for 30-35 minutes.
Serve with a tossed green salad.

Veal in Sour Cream

Time: 1 hour 15 minutes
Serves: 4

1½ lb boned shoulder of veal
2 tablespoons (1 oz) seasoned flour
3 rashers bacon
2 onions
2 oz butter or margarine
1 teaspoon paprika pepper
salt and pepper
1 tablespoon vinegar
½ cup water
1 tablespoon tomato paste
1 green capsicum
1x6¾ oz can champignons, drained
½ pint sour cream
boiled rice or new potatoes for serving

Chop veal into 1½-inch pieces, dip in seasoned flour. Remove rind from bacon and chop. Peel onions and chop finely.

Heat butter in a flameproof casserole and add bacon and onion, cook until onion is transparent. Add veal and stirring occasionally, cook until well browned. Add paprika pepper, salt and pepper to taste, vinegar, water and tomato paste. Bring to the boil, reduce heat, cover and simmer for 1 hour or until veal is tender.

Meanwhile, seed capsicum and slice finely. Add capsicum, champignons and sour cream to casserole and simmer gently, uncovered, for a further 15 minutes.

Serve with boiled rice or new potatoes.

Veal and Pork Casserole

Time: approximately 1¾ hours
Temperature: 350-375° F
Serves: 6

1 lb boned shoulder of veal
1 lb lean belly pork
2 tablespoons oil
2 tablespoons caraway seeds
1x15 oz can sauerkraut
1x1 lb jar red cabbage pickle
1 teaspoon salt
1½ cups sour cream
1 teaspoon paprika pepper for garnish
boiled potatoes for serving

Trim gristle and excess fat from meat, cut into 1½-inch pieces.

Heat oil in a flameproof casserole, brown meat evenly all over. Add caraway seeds and mix together. Add drained sauerkraut, red cabbage and salt. Cover and cook in a moderate oven for approximately 1½ hours or until meat is tender. Remove from oven, add sour cream and mix thoroughly, adjust seasoning if necessary. Replace in oven for 15 minutes.

Sprinkle with paprika pepper and serve with boiled potatoes.

Kidneys in Burgundy

A delicious supper dish.

Time: approximately 30 minutes
Temperature: 350-375° F
Serves: 6

12 lambs' kidneys
2 oz butter or margarine
1 tablespoon (½ oz) plain flour
3 tablespoons finely chopped parsley
1 clove garlic, crushed
1 cup Burgundy
¼ cup water
salt and pepper
hot buttered toast for serving

Soak kidneys in salted water for 30 minutes. Skin and cut in halves, remove white core.

Heat butter in a flameproof casserole, sauté kidneys quickly to seal in the juices. Sprinkle with flour and blend in smoothly. Add parsley, garlic, wine and water. Stirring continuously, bring to the boil. Season to taste with salt and pepper.

Cover casserole and cook in a moderate oven for approximately 30 minutes. Serve kidneys with fingers of hot buttered toast.

Curried Chicken

Time: approximately 45 minutes
Temperature: 350-375° F
Serves: 4

1x3 lb chicken
2 oz butter or margarine
2 onions, chopped
1 tablespoon curry powder
1 teaspoon curry paste
1 tablespoon (½ oz) plain flour
2 cups chicken stock or water and chicken stock cubes
1 clove garlic, crushed
salt and pepper
1 tablespoon redcurrant jelly
½ cup Coconut Milk (see below)
¼ cup cream
boiled rice and chutney for serving

Cut chicken into serving pieces. Melt butter in a flameproof casserole and fry chicken pieces until golden brown, remove from casserole and sauté onion in remaining fat until golden. Add curry powder and paste and continue to cook for 3-4 minutes. Add flour and blend until smooth. Stirring continuously, add stock and bring to the boil. Replace chicken in casserole, add garlic and season to taste with salt and pepper.

Cover casserole and cook in moderate oven for approximately 45 minutes or until chicken is tender. Place chicken on a serving dish and keep warm. Add redcurrant jelly and coconut milk to curry sauce, bring to the boil and simmer 5 minutes. Add cream and spoon sauce over chicken pieces.

Serve curry with boiled rice and chutney.

Coconut Milk: Pour ½ cup boiling water over 1 large tablespoon desiccated coconut. Stand for 1 hour. Strain before using.

Party Chicken

Time: approximately 1 hour
Temperature: 350-375° F
Serves: 4-6

8 oz spaghetti
2x10 oz cans asparagus tips
4 oz butter or margarine
1 cup (4 oz) plain flour
2 pints combined chicken stock and asparagus liquid
½ teaspoon salt
freshly ground pepper
pinch of nutmeg
2 tablespoons whipped cream
2 tablespoons dry sherry
4 cups diced cooked chicken
½ cup fine dry breadcrumbs
¼ cup grated Parmesan cheese

Break spaghetti into short pieces and cook in boiling salted water until tender. Rinse and drain well. Drain asparagus tips, reserve liquid and cut into 1-inch pieces.

Melt butter in a saucepan, add flour and blend until smooth. Add chicken stock and stirring continuously, bring to the boil. Season to taste with salt, pepper and nutmeg. Add cream and sherry.

Place spaghetti in a large greased ovenproof casserole. Cover with a little sauce and arrange chicken and asparagus on top. Cover with remaining sauce and top with breadcrumbs and greated cheese.

Cook in a moderate oven for approximately 1 hour or until hot and golden brown on top.

Salmis of Duck

Time: 2 hours
Temperature: 400-450° F
    reducing to 350-375° F
Serves: 4

1x3 lb duck
2 tablespoons dripping
¼ pint port wine
fried croûtes, stuffed green olives and sautéed button
mushrooms for garnish

Espagnole Sauce:
2 oz lard
2 onions, roughly chopped
2 carrots, roughly chopped
2 rashers bacon, chopped
4 tablespoons (2 oz) plain flour
1 pint water
1 beef or chicken stock cube
2 tomatoes, roughly chopped
4 oz mushrooms, roughly chopped
bouquet garni
salt and pepper

Place duck in a roasting pan with dripping and roast in a hot
oven for 1 hour.

Cut duck into neat joints and place in a large ovenproof
casserole. Add espagnole sauce, cover and cook in a moderate
oven for a further 1 hour or until duck is tender. Add port
wine and adjust seasoning if necessary. Garnish with fried
croûtes, olives and sautéed mushrooms before serving. Serve
with a citrus salad.

Espagnole Sauce: Melt lard in a heavy based saucepan, fry
onion, carrot and bacon until golden brown. Remove all but
2 tablespoons of fat from saucepan. Add flour and stirring
continuously, cook for 5-10 minutes until golden brown. Add
all remaining ingredients, cover and simmer gently for
approximately 1 hour. Strain before using.

Rabbit with Prunes

Ideal for a cold winter day.

Time: approximately 1 hour
Serves: 4

8 oz prunes, stoned
1 young rabbit
3 tablespoons (1½ oz) plain flour
1½ oz butter or margarine
½ cup red wine
1½ cups beef stock or water and beef stock cubes
salt and pepper

Place prunes in a bowl, cover with cold water and soak overnight.

Wipe rabbit thoroughly with a damp cloth and cut into serving pieces, dip in flour.

Melt butter in a flameproof casserole and brown rabbit on all sides, add wine, stock and salt and pepper to taste. Cover casserole and simmer gently for 30 minutes, add drained prunes and simmer for a further 30 minutes or until rabbit is tender.

Serve with a green vegetable and creamed potato.

Curried Fish

Time: 35 minutes
Temperature: 350-375° F
Serves: 3-4

2 tablespoons desiccated coconut
¾ pint fish stock or water
1 apple
2 oz butter or margarine
1 onion, sliced
2 spring onions, chopped
2 tablespoons (1 oz) plain flour
1 tablespoon curry powder
1 tablespoon fruit chutney
1 lb fish fillets (snapper or flathead)
squeeze of lemon juice
1 tablespoon redcurrant jelly
salt
pinch of cayenne pepper
wedges of lemon and finely chopped parsley for garnish
boiled rice for serving

Place coconut in a bowl, pour over stock and stand aside for
20 minutes.

Peel, core and chop apple. Melt butter in a flameproof
casserole, add onion, apple and spring onions. Sauté gently for
approximately 5 minutes until golden. Add flour and curry
powder and blend until smooth, cook for a further 3 minutes.
Add chutney and stock and stirring continuously, bring to the
boil, simmer for 5 minutes.

Cut fish into 1-inch pieces, add to sauce in casserole. Cover
and cook in a moderate oven for 30 minutes. Remove from
oven, add lemon juice, redcurrant jelly and season to taste with
salt and cayenne pepper. Mix together thoroughly and return
to oven for a further 5 minutes.

Garnish with wedges of lemon and chopped parsley and serve
with boiled rice.

Snapper in Wine Sauce

Time: 10-15 minutes
Temperature: 350-375° F
Serves: 4

1 oz butter or margarine
4 snapper steaks
salt
freshly ground pepper
slices of lemon and chopped parsley for garnish

Wine Sauce:
2 oz butter or margarine
2 small onions, finely sliced
1 pint dry white wine
bouquet garni
2 tablespoons (1 oz) plain flour

Heat butter in a frying pan, lightly brown snapper on both sides. Season with salt and pepper and place in a shallow greased casserole.

Pour wine sauce over snapper in casserole. Cook in a moderate oven for 10-15 minutes. Garnish with slices of lemon and chopped parsley before serving.

Wine Sauce: Melt half the butter in a saucepan, sauté onion until transparent and tender. Add wine and bouquet garni and boil rapidly until reduced by half, strain.

Melt remaining butter in a saucepan, add flour and blend until smooth. Cook for 2-3 minutes. Add reduced wine and stirring continuously, bring to the boil.

Prawn Créole

Time: 30-40 minutes
Temperature: 350-375° F
Serves: 4

4 oz butter or margarine
1 large onion, finely chopped
1 small capsicum, seeded and finely chopped
1 clove garlic, crushed
1x15 oz can peeled tomatoes
3 tablespoons tomato paste
1 tablespoon Worcestershire sauce
1 teaspoon paprika pepper
pinch of sugar
salt
freshly ground pepper
1½ lb cooked prawns, shelled
2 teaspoons cornflour blended with 1 tablespoon water
boiled rice for serving

Melt butter in a flameproof casserole, sauté onion, capsicum
and garlic until tender. Add tomatoes, tomato paste,
Worcestershire sauce and seasonings, cover. Cook in a moderate
oven for 20-30 minutes. Add prawns and blended cornflour,
mix well and adjust seasonings if necessary. Return to oven for
a further 10 minutes or until prawns are hot. Serve with boiled
rice.

Note: When using raw prawns, return casserole to oven for
20-30 minutes or until prawns are cooked.

Scallop Mornay

Time: approximately 20 minutes
Temperature: 375-400° F
Serves: 4

1 lb scallops
2 tablespoons grated Parmesan cheese
½ cup soft white breadcrumbs

Sauce:
1½ oz butter or margarine
1 small onion, chopped
3 tablespoons (1½ oz) plain flour
2 cups milk
salt
pinch of cayenne pepper
1/3 cup grated tasty cheese
1 tablespoon lemon juice

Clean scallops by washing thoroughly in salted water, drain. Combine scallops and sauce and pour into a greased ovenproof casserole. Sprinkle with grated Parmesan cheese and breadcrumbs.

Cook in a moderately hot oven for approximately 20 minutes or until lightly brown on top. Serve immediately.

Sauce: Melt butter in a saucepan and sauté onion until transparent and tender. Add flour and mix until smooth. Add milk and stirring continuously, bring to the boil. Simmer 3-4 minutes. Add salt to taste, cayenne pepper, grated cheese and lemon juice. Remove from heat and stir until cheese has melted.

Noté: Do not overcook as scallops will become tough.

Alternative: 'Thatch' top of casserole with de-rinded bacon rashers before placing in oven. Serve when bacon is crisp and golden brown.

INTERNATIONAL CASSEROLES

Casseroles collected from around the globe
can be made equally well at home. From the
simple Irish Stew to deliciously rich Beef à la
Bourgignonne, these dishes remind you of
holidays overseas. Make them often for
small informal gatherings and more formal
dinners—there are many ideas here.

Beef à la Bourguignonne

An ideal party casserole.

Time: approximately 2 hours'
Temperature: 350-375° F
Serves: 4-5

2 lb lean topside steak
salt and pepper
1 large onion, sliced
bouquet garni
¼ pint red wine
2 tablespoons olive oil
4 oz salted belly pork
2 tablespoons dripping
8 small white onions
2 tablespoons (1 oz) seasoned flour
½ pint beef stock or water and beef stock cube
1 clove garlic, crushed
8 oz button mushrooms
1 oz butter or margarine

Cut steak into 1½-inch pieces, place in a bowl with salt and pepper, onion, bouquet garni, red wine and olive oil. Cover and marinate for 3-6 hours.

Cut pork into ¼-inch pieces. Heat dripping in a heavy based ovenproof casserole, add pork and small white onions and sauté until golden brown on all sides, remove from casserole. Drain meat thoroughly, toss in seasoned flour and brown in remaining fat. Add strained marinade and boil for half a minute. Add stock, bouquet garni and garlic. Cover casserole and cook in a moderate oven for approximately 1½ hours.

Meanwhile, in a small saucepan, sauté mushrooms for approximately 5 minutes in butter. Return pork, onions and mushrooms to casserole and cook for a further 30 minutes. Remove bouquet garni before serving.

Note: For a cheaper dish, use chuck steak and allow an extra 45 minutes cooking time.

Beef Curry

Time: approximately 2 hours
Temperature: 350-375° F
Serves: 4-5

1½ lb blade steak
2 tablespoons (1 oz) seasoned flour
2 tablespoons oil
2 tablespoons curry powder
1 clove garlic, crushed
2 large onions, thinly sliced
2 tablespoons jam or fruit chutney
1 cup beef stock or water and beef stock cube
boiled rice for serving

Trim meat and cut into 1-inch pieces. Coat with seasoned flour.

Heat oil in a flameproof casserole, add curry powder, garlic and onion, sauté for approximately 5 minutes, stirring occasionally. Add meat and brown lightly. Add jam and stock, bring to the boil and mix thoroughly.

Cover casserole and cook in a moderate oven for approximately 2 hours or until meat is tender. Serve with boiled rice.

Note: A variety of accompaniments can make curry an ideal party dish. Serve sliced cucumber in sour cream, tomato wedges, finely chopped onion, chutney, peanuts or almonds, pineapple pieces, sultanas, toasted coconut, sliced banana or poppadums.

RAGOÛT OF BEEF
(see page 94)

SELECTION OF CASSEROLES

Beef à la Mode

A traditional French stew.

Time: 3-3½ hours
Serves: 5-6

2 onions
1 lb carrots
1 clove garlic
4 lb unsalted silverside
½ cup red wine
1¼ cups water
salt and pepper
1 clove (optional)
8 oz pork rind
1 veal foreshank
horseradish relish and sautéed potatoes for serving

Slice onions, carrots and garlic, place in a large bowl with beef, wine, water, salt and pepper and clove if used. Cover bowl and marinate for approximately 8 hours or overnight, turn occasionally.

Cut pork rind into pieces and place in a fireproof casserole, add all ingredients except carrots. Cover casserole, bring to the boil, lower heat and simmer very gently for 3-3½ hours. Add carrots 1 hour before cooking time is completed.

Carve silverside and serve with a little of the well flavoured stock. Accompany with horseradish relish and sautéed potatoes.

Goulash and Noodles

Time: approximately 2 hours
Temperature: 350-375° F
Serves: 6

2 oz butter or margarine
3 onions, chopped
1 green capsicum, seeded and chopped
1 clove garlic, crushed
2 lb blade steak
2 tablespoons (1 oz) plain flour
1½ teaspoons salt
pinch of pepper
4 beef stock cubes dissolved in 2 cups boiling water
½ teaspoon paprika pepper
12 oz French beans, sliced
2 carrots, sliced

Poppy Seed Noodles:
8 oz noodles
1½ tablespoons poppy seeds
1 oz butter

In a heavy based flameproof casserole, heat half the butter.
Sauté onion, capsicum and garlic until onion is transparent,
remove from casserole.

Cut meat into 1-1½-inch pieces and toss in flour seasoned with
salt and pepper. Melt remaining butter in casserole and lightly
brown meat, add stock, sautéed vegetables and pepper paprika.
Mix thoroughly, cover and cook in a moderate oven for
approximately 1½ hours.

Add prepared beans and carrots. Cover and cook for a further
30 minutes or until meat and carrots are tender. Serve with
poppy seed noodles.

Poppy Seed Noodles: Cook noodles in boiling salted water for
12-15 minutes or until tender. Drain, add poppy seeds and
butter, toss together gently and serve immediately with
goulash.

Moussaka

Time: 30-45 minutes
Temperature: 350-375° F
Serves: 4

2 tablespoons oil
1 lb minced steak
2 large onions, finely chopped
1 lb tomatoes, skinned and chopped
salt
freshly ground pepper
1 small eggplant
extra ¼ cup oil
4 tablespoons dry white wine

Cheese Sauce:
1 oz butter or margarine
2 tablespoons (1 oz) plain flour
½ pint milk
salt and pepper
2-3 oz tasty cheese, grated
2 eggs, separated

Heat oil in a saucepan and fry meat until brown, add onions,
tomatoes and salt and pepper. Mix together thoroughly and
simmer for 10-15 minutes.

Meanwhile, slice eggplant thickly and sauté in extra oil until
tender. Alternate layers of eggplant and meat mixture in a
greased ovenproof casserole. Sprinkle with wine.

Pour cheese sauce over casserole and bake in a moderate oven
for 30-40 minutes or until hot and golden brown on top. Serve
with a tossed green salad.

Cheese Sauce: Melt butter in a saucepan, blend in flour until
smooth. Add milk and stirring continuously, bring to the boil.
Season to taste with salt and pepper. Remove sauce from heat,
add cheese, stir until melted. Add beaten egg yolks. Whisk
egg whites until stiff and gently fold into sauce.

Sauerbraten

Time: 2½-3 hours
Temperature: 350-375° F
Serves: 6

1x4 lb rolled sirloin of beef
¾ pint dry red wine
¼ pint red wine vinegar
1 teaspoon salt
1 teaspoon black peppercorns
2 large onions, sliced
2 large carrots, sliced
2 stalks celery, chopped
½ lemon, sliced
2 bay leaves
4 sprigs parsley
4 allspice berries
4 cloves
3 oz butter or margarine
4 tablespoons (2 oz) plain flour
1 tablespoon (½ oz) brown sugar
buttered noodles for serving

Place meat in a deep bowl. In a saucepan combine wine, wine
vinegar, salt, peppercorns, onions, carrots, celery, lemon, bay
leaves, parsley, allspice and cloves. Bring to the boil and pour
over meat. Cover and place in refrigerator for 3 days, turn
meat each day.

Remove meat from marinade, wipe dry. Heat 2 oz of the
butter in a flameproof casserole. Sprinkle half the flour over
meat and brown all over in hot butter.

Meanwhile, heat marinade and pour over meat. Cover tightly
and place casserole in a moderate oven for 2½-3 hours or until
meat is tender. Take meat out of marinade and keep in a warm
place. Strain marinade.

Melt remaining butter in a saucepan, blend in remaining flour
and sugar until smooth, cook until lightly browned. Add
marinade and stirring continuously, bring to the boil. Simmer
for 5 minutes.

Carve meat and arrange on a serving plate, pour some sauce
over. Serve remaining sauce in a gravy boat. Serve Sauerbraten
with buttered noodles.

Lasagna

Time: approximately 30 minutes
Temperature: 350-375° F
Serves: 6-8

8 oz green lasagna
2 tablespoons oil
2 lb minced steak
2 cloves garlic, crushed
½ cup chopped onion
salt
freshly ground pepper
1x8 oz can tomato paste
2 oz butter or margarine
½ cup (2 oz) plain flour
1½ cups milk
extra salt and pepper
½ cup dry white wine
¼ cup finely chopped parsley
1x6¾ oz can button mushrooms, sliced
8 oz ricotta cheese
½ cup grated Parmesan cheese

Cook lasagna in boiling salted water until tender, drain and rinse thoroughly.

Heat oil in a large frying pan and brown minced steak, add garlic, onion, seasonings and tomato paste. Mix together thoroughly. Melt butter in a saucepan, blend in flour until smooth. Add milk and stirring continuously, bring to the boil, season to taste with salt and pepper. Add wine, parsley and mushrooms, mix thoroughly.

Pour approximately half cup of the white sauce into a greased ovenproof casserole. Cover with a layer of lasagna and half the meat mixture, top with spoonfuls of ricotta cheese. Pour half the remaining white sauce over and repeat the layers, finishing with sauce. Sprinkle top with Parmesan cheese. Bake in a moderate oven for approximately 30 minutes or until hot and golden brown on top.

Note: Plain lasagna may be used instead of green.

117

Osso Bucco

Time: 1½-2 hours
Temperature: 350-375° F
Serves: 4

4 shins of veal
salt and pepper
2 oz butter or margarine
4 carrots, chopped
2 stalks celery, chopped
2 tablespoons (1 oz) plain flour
1½ cups canned tomatoes
½ cup red wine
veal stock or water and beef stock cube
sprig of fresh thyme
1 bay leaf
finely chopped parsley for garnish
boiled rice for serving

Ask the butcher to cut veal shins into 2-inch pieces across the leg bone.

Season meat with salt and pepper. Melt butter in a flameproof casserole, add meat and brown lightly. Add prepared vegetables and stirring occasionally, cook until vegetables are golden brown. Add flour and mix in thoroughly. Add tomatoes, wine, just enough stock to cover meat, thyme and bay leaf.

Cover and cook in a moderate oven for 1½-2 hours or until meat is tender. Adjust seasoning if necessary and sprinkle with parsley. Serve with boiled rice.

French Lamb Stew

Time: approximately 1½ hours
Temperature: 350-375° F
Serves: 6

½ cup raisins
2 oz butter or margarine
12 lean lamb cutlets
6 large onions, sliced
3-4 cloves garlic, crushed
2 lb tomatoes, skinned and quartered
1x5 oz can tomato paste
3 large cooking apples, quartered, cored and peeled
salt and pepper

Soak raisins in cold water for 2 hours, drain.

Heat butter in a flameproof casserole and brown cutlets evenly on both sides. Add onions, garlic, tomatoes, tomato paste, raisins, apples and salt and pepper to taste. Cover casserole and simmer gently in a moderate oven for approximately 1½ hours or until meat is tender. Adjust seasoning if necessary before serving.

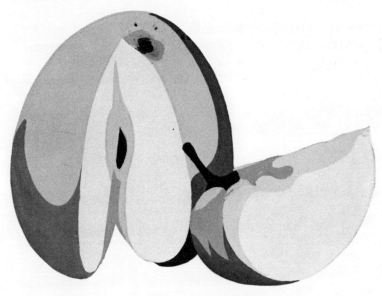

Irish Stew

Time: 2-2½ hours
Temperature: 325-350° F
Serves: 5-6

2 lb best end neck chops
2 lb potatoes
1 lb white onions
salt and pepper
bunch of herbs
1 bay leaf
1 pint stock or water and stock cubes
1 tablespoon finely chopped parsley for serving

Trim excess fat from chops. Peel potatoes, cut 3-4 potatoes into thick slices and cut remaining potatoes in halves. Peel and thickly slice onions.

Place sliced potatoes in an ovenproof casserole, season with salt and pepper. Cover with meat and finally add onions and halved potatoes, season with salt and pepper. Add herbs, bay leaf and stock.

Cover casserole tightly and cook in a moderately slow oven for 2-2½ hours or until meat is tender. Remove herbs and bay leaf from casserole and sprinkle with chopped parsley before serving.

Sauerkraut Garni

This famous dish originated in Germany, there are many variations.

Time: 2 hours
Temperature: 350-375° F
Serves: 4

1½ lb salted belly pork
1 onion, sliced
1 carrot, sliced
1 lb sauerkraut
¼ cup chicken stock or water and chicken stock cube
freshly ground black pepper
2 knackwurst sausages
2 frankfurters
Beurre Marnié (see below)
chopped parsley for garnish
boiled potatoes for serving

Place pork in a saucepan, cover with water and simmer for 1 hour, cool in liquid.

Place prepared onion and carrot in a greased ovenproof casserole. Pull the sauerkraut apart with 2 forks and place half in the casserole. Place pork on top and cover with remaining sauerkraut. Add stock and pepper, cover casserole. Place in moderate oven and cook for 1 hour. Meanwhile, cook sausages and frankfurters in simmering water for 5 minutes. Drain and cut into thick slices, keep warm.

Remove pork from casserole, slice and keep warm. Place casserole over heat and bind sauerkraut with beurre marnié.

To serve, pile sauerkraut in centre of serving dish, top with slices of pork and surround with sliced sausages and frankfurters. Garnish with chopped parsley and serve with boiled potatoes.

Beurre Marnié: Blend 1½ oz softened butter or margarine with 1 tablespoon (½ oz) plain flour, mix to a smooth paste. Add to casserole in small pieces, stirring continuously.

Chicken Cacciatora

Time: approximately 1½ hours
Temperature: 350-375° F
Serves: 4

1x3 lb chicken
4 tablespoons olive oil
2 onions, sliced
1x16 oz can peeled tomatoes
1 cup tomato sauce
salt
freshly ground pepper
1-2 cloves garlic, crushed
½ teaspoon celery seed
½ teaspoon dried oregano
1 bay leaf

Joint chicken into serving pieces.

Heat oil in a flameproof casserole and brown chicken pieces.
Remove from casserole and sauté onion in remaining oil until
golden and tender.

Add remaining ingredients and mix thoroughly. Replace
chicken pieces in casserole, cover and cook in a moderate oven
for approximately 1½ hours or until chicken is tender. Remove
bay leaf before serving.

Coq au Vin

Time: 45 minutes
Temperature: 350-375° F
Serves: 4

1x3 lb chicken
1 tablespoon oil
2 oz butter or margarine
4 rashers bacon
4 small onions
2 tablespoons brandy
1½ cups Burgundy
2 oz button mushrooms (optional)
2 cloves garlic, crushed
bouquet garni
salt and pepper
Beurre Manié (see below)
chopped parsley and fried croûtes of bread for garnish

Cut chicken into serving pieces. Heat oil and butter in a flame-proof casserole, brown chicken and remove. Cut rind from bacon and chop, add to casserole with onions and sauté until golden brown. Replace chicken in casserole. Pour over warm brandy, ignite. Add Burgundy, mushrooms if used, garlic, bouquet garni and salt and pepper to taste.

Cover casserole and cook in a moderate oven for approximately 45 minutes or until chicken is tender. Remove bouquet garni and thicken casserole slightly with beurre manié, adjust seasoning if necessary and garnish with chopped parsley and fried croûtes of bread before serving.

Beurre Manié: Blend ½ oz softened butter or margarine with 1 tablespoon (½ oz) plain flour, mix to a smooth paste. Add to casserole in small pieces, stirring continuously.

Duck and Pineapple Canton

Time: 1 hour
Serves: 4

1x4 lb duck
¼ cup soya sauce
3 tablespoons (1½ oz) sugar
1 piece root ginger, finely chopped
¼ cup oil
2 cups water
1 cup pineapple syrup, drained from canned pineapple pieces
1 clove garlic, crushed
1 teaspoon salt
3 tablespoons (1½ oz) cornflour mixed to a smooth paste
    with ¼ cup water
2 cups canned pineapple pieces
boiled rice for serving

Wipe duck thoroughly with a damp cloth and cut into serving pieces. In a bowl, combine soya sauce, sugar and ginger. Dip pieces of duck into mixture. Heat oil in a flameproof casserole and fry pieces of duck until well browned on all sides. Add water, pineapple syrup, garlic and salt. Cover casserole and simmer gently for 1 hour or until duck is tender.

Remove duck from casserole and keep warm. Add blended cornflour and pineapple pieces to casserole and stirring continuously, bring to the boil, simmer for 5 minutes.

Pour sauce over duck and serve immediately with boiled rice.

Ratatouille

Time: approximately 1 hour
Temperature: 350-375° F
Serves: 6-8

4 tablespoons olive oil
2 cloves garlic, crushed
1 lb eggplant, thinly sliced
2 lb tomatoes, thinly sliced
1 lb zucchini, thinly sliced
3 green capsicums, seeded and thinly sliced
1 cup white wine or water
salt
freshly ground pepper
pinch of sugar

Heat oil in a large heavy based frying pan and brown
vegetables in turn, cooking quickly and placing them in an
ovenproof casserole as they brown, (add extra olive oil if
necessary). When all vegetables are browned, add wine and
seasonings to taste.

Cover casserole and cook in a moderate oven for approximately 1 hour or until vegetables are tender. Adjust seasonings
if necessary and serve hot as a vegetable or cold as an
hors d'oeuvre.

Acknowledgements

ACKNOWLEDGEMENTS

The editor would like to thank the following for their
assistance in providing information and equipment for
Casserole Cookbook

Corning Glass Works
Incorporated Agencies Pty. Ltd.
Lawry's Foods International (Inc.)
Malleys Limited
New Theme Pty. Ltd. and Etcetera, Sydney
The Bay Tree Kitchen Shop, Woollahra
Maurice Tattersall, Head Teacher, Food School,
    Meat Division, East Sydney Technical College.

Index